"You've got a great message, you ha
when you speak—now go get paid wh
Jeff will show you how to master th;
cessful speaker."

John Jantsch, au
and .

"The business of speaking can feel overwhelming when you're just getting started. Grant Baldwin and Jeff Goins have produced the most comprehensive guide I've found for identifying your core message, shaping it, and getting on stages to present it. If you want to develop a speaking career, there's no better place to start."

Todd Henry, author of *Herding Tigers*

"Few career paths can be as daunting as that of a professional speaker. Thankfully, Grant has given us this manual detailing what to focus on, what to ignore, and ultimately how to find success as a speaker."

Dan Miller, *New York Times* bestselling author of *48 Days to the Work You Love*

"The best roadmaps are created by those who charted their own path. Grant tells you how he did it and then guides you on your journey every step of the way."

Chris Ducker, founder of youpreneur.com

"Speaking is an incredible way to impact the masses—and leave a lasting legacy. In *The Successful Speaker*, Baldwin artfully breaks down the tools, strategies, and systems required to build a profitable career that serves your people and your purpose."

Nicole Walters, TV personality and CEO of Inherit Learning Company

"If you are just starting to consider a career in speaking or you have given a few speeches but want to take your efforts to the next level, this book is required reading. Baldwin outlines an easy-to-follow, step-by-step process for creating your speech, building your brand, and growing your business. If you want to be a successful speaker, this is the book for you."

Joey Coleman, award-winning keynote speaker and *Wall Street Journal* bestselling author of *Never Lose a Customer Again*

"If you've ever wondered whether a career in public speaking is right for you, this book is an excellent introduction. Grant doesn't sugarcoat the work that is required, but his simple plan for finding and booking gigs is something anyone can put into practice."

Michael Port, cofounder of Heroic Public Speaking Worldwide
and *New York Times* and *Wall Street Journal*
bestselling author of *Steal the Show*

"I wish I had this book fifteen years ago when I started my speaking career. It would have saved me fifteen years of mistakes. Read Grant's book by today, and start doing what he teaches by yesterday."

Mike Michalowicz, author of *Clockwork*, *Profit First*,
and *The Pumpkin Plan*

"This book is an excellent primer for anyone wondering how to get started in the world of professional speaking. Baldwin and Goins have written a concise and useful guide that will save you time and set you on your way."

Mark Sanborn, award-winning speaker, bestselling author,
and president of Sanborn & Associates, Inc.

"Being a professional speaker is a lone-wolf industry. We're all making it up as we go, learning from our own mistakes and what-ifs, and debating getting 'real' jobs every time we peek at next year's calendar. This book changes all of that. This would be the completed notebook you'd cherish if you went on the road with one hundred speakers simultaneously. Never have both the craft *and* the business of speaking been covered together in one book."

Scott Stratten, CPAE Hall of Fame inductee
and full-time keynote speaker

"Simply put, Grant's insights on the speaking biz are a game-changer. There's a lot of clutter out there, and speakers need to focus their energy in the right places. Luckily, Grant separates the signal from the noise and shows you where to put your focus every step along the way. If you want to be a successful public speaker, listen to Grant and read this book."

Ron Tite, bestselling author, speaker, and founder
of Church+State

"Giving a speech is easy. Getting paid to give a speech is much harder, which is why this book is so valuable. A must-read for every emerging speaker, it'll save you years of trial and error."

Jay Baer, Hall of Fame speaker and coauthor of *Talk Triggers*

"This is the manual for the total business of professional speaking. I wish this book was available when I started my career."

David Burkus, author of *Friend of a Friend*

"A must-read for anyone who wants to maximize their time and energy building a career as a speaker."

Tim Sanders, *New York Times* bestselling author of *Love Is the Killer App: How to Win Business and Influence Friends*

"If you want to be a public speaker, whether as your full-time job or just as a hobby, this is the book you need, and Grant Baldwin has been there and done that. Every page offers insight, hope, and practical advice for anyone who wants to spread their message. Grant's conversational tone and years of hard-earned know-how make him the perfect guide."

Hal Elrod, international keynote speaker and bestselling author of *The Miracle Morning* and *The Miracle Equation*

"Becoming a public speaker is accessible to anyone willing to put in the work. If you want to stand out and skip the silly mistakes along the way, read this book immediately. Grant makes the journey so much easier with his five simple steps on the road to speaking success."

Amy Schmittauer Landino, public speaker, author of *Vlog Like a Boss*, and creator of the award-winning YouTube series AmyTV

"To create a thriving speaking career, you need two things: a captivating message and a consistent system. This book will teach you how to create both in a way that makes you stand out! This is a game-changing guide to booking more events and making a bigger impact."

Shawn Stevenson, international bestselling author of *Sleep Smarter*

"Finally, a great book about public speaking that tells it like it is. Grant provides the practical, roll-up-your-sleeves approach that's needed for up-and-coming speakers. He not only shows you exactly what to do but encourages you to have fun and not take yourself too seriously along the way. Grab this book now and you're sure to propel your career as a speaker."

Pat Flynn, *Wall Street Journal* bestselling author of *Will It Fly?* and founder of SmartPassiveIncome.com

"Going from person with a big idea to paid speaker on a big stage feels totally overwhelming and confusing to most people. Grant breaks down his road-tested methodology in a clear and actionable manner that will get you paid gigs. This book is worth every penny, and you need to read every page."

Pamela Slim, author of *Body of Work*

"Good grief. I only *wish* I had this information when I started on my road to becoming a professional speaker ten years ago. Grant Baldwin has finally laid out a true plan and system for anyone wishing for more stages to get momentum and achieve their dreams to change the lives of others through their words. Highly recommend!"

Marcus Sheridan, full-time professional speaker

"I was hoping that Grant and Jeff would not write this book. Guys, this business is supposed to be a secret! One of the greatest ways to make a living is to speak. The problem is that everyone thinks that they can speak. Imagine saying 'I want to be brain surgeon!' You would have to go to school, study, work hard, and maybe (just maybe) you would become a doctor. For some reason, people think that speaking doesn't require any training, skill, or knowledge. It does. Especially if you want to do it well. With *The Successful Speaker*, you now have the manual and roadmap for how to make it happen. Speaking isn't brain surgery, but if you want to make a living at it, you need to study the skill and work at the practice as if it were. Here's where to (really) start. See you on the stage."

Mitch Joel, author of *Six Pixels of Separation* and *Ctrl Alt Delete*

"Experts these days are a dime a dozen. The credibility isn't in the teaching, the credibility is in the living. Grant Baldwin is one of the rare experts out there whose content is backed by real-world results. If you want to start, run, and grow a professional speaking business, this is the book for you."

Mike Kim, brand strategist and copywriter

"The speaking business is a magical and life-changing industry for both audiences *and* speakers. Grant delivers a practical, nononsense guide to joining the greatest profession in the world!"

Phil Jones, professional speaker and author of *Exactly What to Say*

THE SUCCESSFUL SPEAKER

THE SUCCESSFUL SPEAKER

FIVE STEPS FOR **BOOKING GIGS**, **GETTING PAID**, AND **BUILDING YOUR PLATFORM**

GRANT BALDWIN
WITH JEFF GOINS

© 2023 by Grant Baldwin

Printed in the United States of America

All rights reserved. No part of this publication may be reproduced, stored in a retrieval system, or transmitted in any form or by any means—for example, electronic, photocopy, recording—without the prior written permission of the publisher. The only exception is brief quotations in printed reviews.

Library of Congress Cataloging-in-Publication Data
Names: Baldwin, Grant, author.
Title: The successful speaker : five steps for booking gigs, getting paid, and building your platform / Grant Baldwin, with Jeff Goins.
Identifiers: ISBN 979-885207105-7
Subjects: LCSH: Public speaking—Vocational guidance.
Classification: LCC PN4098 .B35 2020 | DDC 808.5/1023—dc23
LC record available at https://lccn.loc.gov/2019026735

This book is dedicated to speakers everywhere
who desire to make an impact.
The world needs your message.
You can do this.

CONTENTS

Author's Note   13

Introduction: *How I Became a Speaker*   14

About This Book: *What's in It and Who Is This Guy?*   19

The Speaker Success Roadmap: *Five Steps to Becoming a Successful Speaker*   24

STEP 1   SELECT A PROBLEM TO SOLVE   29

1. Choose an Industry   33
2. Identify an Interest   45
3. Speak with Integrity   58

STEP 2   PREPARE AND DELIVER YOUR TALK   65

4. How to Pick the Right Type of Talk   67
5. How to Create a Great Talk   82
6. What to Do before You Step Onstage   99
7. How to Use Technology and Other Tools   116

CONTENTS

8. How to Deliver a Talk without Boring Your Audience to Tears   131
9. What to Do after You're Done   151

STEP 3 ESTABLISH YOUR EXPERTISE   159

10. Developing a Speaker Brand   161
11. Getting a Great Demo Video   170
12. Setting Up Your Speaker Website   176

STEP 4 ACQUIRE PAID SPEAKING GIGS   185

13. Finding Paid Speaking Gigs   187
14. Reaching Out to Potential Clients   203
15. Closing the Deal   218
16. Customer Service and Repeat Business   232

STEP 5 KNOW WHEN TO SCALE   243

17. Diversifying Your Income Streams   245
18. Creating Your First Product   257
19. Selling from Stage and Other Ways to Monetize   268

Conclusion   275

Acknowledgments   278

AUTHOR'S NOTE

Throughout this book, I share resources, tools, and tips on how to become a professional speaker. I did my best to make these references as helpful as possible. Since technology changes so often, I decided to keep the most up-to-date resources on a separate website, which I'll refer to at the end of each chapter, and in a few other places throughout the book when relevant. On this website, I've also included links to free resources and a current list of the best tools for building your brand and business as a speaker.

You can find this list of resources, tools, and other free bonuses at SpeakerBookBonus.com.

INTRODUCTION

How I Became a Speaker

In 2006 my wife, Sheila, and I decided to pursue a dream. We had no savings, had just left a stable position at a church where I was serving as the youth pastor, and—oh, yeah—our first daughter, Sydnee, had just been born. We were newlyweds, recent college graduates, and brand-new parents. After we left the church job with no firm career plans, our friends and family were asking what we were going to do about money and health insurance, and in retrospect those were pretty good questions.

Because we had no idea.

Sheila was learning how to be a mom for the first time, while I held down a few part-time jobs as a security guard and waiter to make ends meet. On the side I was moonlighting as a public speaker, a job for which I had yet to be paid, so I guess you couldn't really call it a job. It was more like a really cool idea that was becoming less cool every single day.

INTRODUCTION

For over a year, I juggled too many things and prayed nothing would come crashing to the ground. My wife was hanging in there, but we were both getting tired of the juggling act, and I knew things couldn't continue this way much longer. Something had to change, or I'd have to give up my dream. My wife had been patient, but time and money were running out, and we were both close to giving up.

In those days, I would reach out to anyone I could think of who might want to book me as a speaker. To my surprise, one of those emails received a reply that didn't start with "please remove me from your list." The event planner of a nearby 4-H conference wanted me to speak about leadership to a group of a few hundred students. The event was only a few hours from where I lived, so I gratefully accepted.

The night before the conference, I drove to the venue, checked in to my hotel room, where there was a gift basket waiting for me, and thought, "So this is how it's going to be from now on. This is my new life. Gift baskets and hotel rooms galore." I went to bed blissfully ignorant of the long and hard road that lay ahead of me.

The next day I woke up, ate breakfast, and made my way to the convention center. Many young people are skeptical of motivational speakers, and this group was no different. I was nervous and unsure of myself, but this was the moment I'd been waiting for. After practicing the speech dozens of times over the previous weeks, now it was time to see if all my work would pay off. Either I'd fall flat on my face—figuratively and perhaps even literally—or this dream just might work. Either way, I'd know if speaking was in the cards for me. As soon as I stepped onstage, standing before four hundred young people, my anxiety faded. It was still there, but I stood and delivered the talk the best I could.

Then, nothing happened. At least not at first. There was just this moment of stillness, and I was left wondering if I'd blown my only chance at being a speaker. Had I rushed the talk? Spoken too quickly? Did I botch the delivery? Was the topic not appropriate? Did I accidentally slip into speaking sloppy sophomore-level Spanish? All these thoughts flashed through my mind in a matter of milliseconds when finally, someone broke the silence and started clapping. It was one at first, then another quickly followed. Then another, and another, and so on until a room full of teenagers and adults were standing on their feet, applauding my speech. I couldn't believe it; my first speaking gig was receiving a standing ovation.

Afterward, students and adults came to thank me, some even inviting me to speak at their upcoming events. Ever since I had been a kid in youth group watching my youth pastor captivate an audience with his words, this had been a dream of mine—to speak for a living—and here I was, actually doing it. On my way out the door, I stopped to see the event planner and thank him for having me, and he handed me an envelope with my name on it. I opened the envelope to see a check for $1,000. Though our contract had been for this amount, all I could do was stare at it, dumbfounded. I may have even drooled a little. *You just paid me $1,000*, I thought, *to run my mouth for forty-five minutes, and it was pure fun.*

Before they decided to change their minds, I hightailed it out of there, escaping the convention center with check in hand, not stopping until I got to my car, where I immediately broke down crying. This wasn't your romantic-comedy

INTRODUCTION

single-tear-on-the-cheek kind of sniffling, by the way. No, it was grab-the-Kleenex-box-and-pause-*Old-Yeller*, full-on, ugly-man weeping. At the time, my family had next to nothing, and we were running on fumes. This was just what we needed to keep going, both emotionally and financially. The moment hit me hard.

Instead of starting the engine and driving home, I sat in the driver's seat for a moment and said to myself, "This is what I want to do. This is what I am meant to do. I know I just made a difference—and they paid me to do it!"

From that point on I knew I wanted to be a speaker. I wanted to travel. I wanted to make an impact. And over the next ten years I did just that, delivering over a thousand presentations, earning more than two million dollars in speaking fees, and speaking to over half a million people. It's been an amazing and unforgettable journey, and I wouldn't trade it for the world.

But let me be clear about something: all those numbers are nice; they're cute and cuddly and make me feel good inside. But I don't share any of them to pat myself on the back. I share all this to say if I can do it, you can do it. If you have a desire to share your message with the world, if you've wondered if this is something you can do, if you're even just a little curious about being a speaker, this book is for you. If you have a message the world needs to hear, then it's up to you to find a way to share it.

In this book, I want to share with you how to do that, along with one very important message: You can be a professional speaker. Not an amateur. Not an "aspiring" speaker. Not someone who fakes it till they make it. The real deal. A successful speaker.

But don't just take my word for it. On this journey of becoming a speaker, I've met hundreds of other successful communicators who have done the same, and they all followed a very specific system. Sure, some of them did this intuitively and others did it intentionally, but what it takes to succeed as a speaker is more than dumb luck. You need a proven process.

In this book I'm going to share that process with you. It's a system I've learned through trial and error, as well as from meeting many speaking mentors along the way. This is the same framework I've been teaching thousands of people over the years whose stories you're going to hear in the coming chapters. These are people who had something to say. People who had a message to share. People just like you.

ABOUT THIS BOOK

What's in It and Who Is This Guy?

What does it mean to be a professional speaker? In a nutshell, it means to start a speaking business. Very few speakers think about this when they get into a speaking career, which is why many fail.

Over the years, people have asked me, "Hey, Grant. I see what you've been doing with your speaking business. How do I do that? How would I go about becoming a speaker?" For the longest time I didn't know how to answer them. One of the great challenges of speaking is that the business part of it can be mysterious. It's one thing to tell you how to deliver a great speech and quite another to tell you what it takes to get your name out there in your respective industry, to get event planners to notice you, and to get booked and paid for that speech.

Professional speaking is an intriguing industry few understand, even those who are in it. In order to get speaking gigs, do you have to be famous? Do you have to write a bestselling book? Do you have to be some "big name" other people know? How does it actually work? The more I heard these questions and attempted to answer them, the more I realized this was a problem I could solve. How *do* you become a successful speaker? To answer the question, I started a podcast called *The Speaker Lab*, where I began interviewing many of the world's most successful speakers and sharing the lessons they've learned about the business and craft of professional speaking. On the show, I share my own experiences as a speaker and the insights I've gained along the way. As listeners of the podcast told me how these stories and lessons resonated with them, I realized what I was sharing was important. The pattern I was starting to see and the process I was starting to teach—how speakers succeed in any industry—wasn't just luck or coincidence. It *worked*.

Eventually, I created other resources to help speakers, including a training program called Booked and Paid to Speak, which thousands of people have used to become successful speakers. In this book you'll get to meet some of them and understand what they did, how they did it, why it worked, and how you can follow in their footsteps to launch your own speaking business.

What's in This Book?

Many people want to become a speaker but don't know how to get started. They feel like they have a message to share, a story to tell, or something important to say. Since you're reading this book, then that probably describes you as well.

And at one point or another, you may have wondered, "Is this even possible? Can I make a living as a speaker?" In this book I'm going to show you my proven process for getting booked and paid to speak. Whether you want to speak a couple of times a year or do it full-time, this book is for you.

Throughout these pages, you'll meet many of my clients, the speakers I've trained over the years, and some of the world's most sought-after communicators. I'll share the system these people have used, which I call the "Speaker Success Roadmap," and how it can help you go from amateur to professional.

I'm confident in this material, not just because I've used it myself, but because I've seen countless others win with it as well. I know it can help you too.

Who Is This Guy?

Before we go any further, I think we should address the elephant in the room: Why should you trust me? You don't know me. We didn't share a room in college or appear in each other's wedding (unless it's you, Brad, reading this, in which case—Hi, Brad!).

In the event that you're not Brad, though, let me just say I'm an ordinary guy. Really. When I started out as a speaker, I didn't have a huge following. I didn't have a "big name." I didn't survive 9/11 or have a *New York Times* bestselling book or land a plane on a major body of water. None of that. I didn't have a massive platform or serve on a presidential cabinet. I didn't survive cancer or climb Everest. Heck, I didn't even have a full head of hair. So what did I have to say? And how could I get people to listen?

What I learned is that being a successful speaker has little to do with any of that. It's more about following a certain set of principles that work again and again, year after year, from industry to industry. As I've seen others apply these same principles and experience success, I've come to trust this process and believe it can work for just about anyone anywhere. In fact, many of my clients have achieved far greater success in their careers than I ever did, which tells me this stuff works. You can trust it.

One more thing before we get started: I know life isn't all about money. Believe me; you don't have to tell me that. I came from a youth ministry background, remember? Do you think I was raking in the big bucks leading a youth group for a small Missouri church? No way. And to be honest, I never did it for the money; speaking was always a passion for me, a calling. However, I knew if I was going to speak for a living, I would need to pay my bills, so money, at some point, was going to have to be part of the equation. That's why that first gig was so important to me. It helped me realize I could get paid to speak and keep doing it. I want you to realize the same. This is not something you have to starve or suffer for; you can make a legitimate income off your message and turn it into a full-time career if you wish. You can be a successful speaker. Whatever success looks like for you, whatever that means in your world, I want to help you build and grow a successful speaking business so you can reach more people and make an impact with your words. I'm thrilled to share this journey with you, helping you wherever you're at, so you can truly succeed and get the rewards your work deserves.

So, yes, we're going to talk about money. We're also going to talk about microphones and speech preparation and travel and all kinds of things. It's a lot, but I promise to make it fun and practical and easy. We'll just take it one step at a time, okay? And here's my final promise: If you do everything in this book, it won't be a question of *if* people start booking you to speak and paying you to do what you love. It'll be a matter of *when*. Now let's get started.

THE SPEAKER SUCCESS ROADMAP

Five Steps to Becoming a Successful Speaker

Imagine you want to take your family on a vacation. If you don't have a family, imagine you and your puppy are going on a trip together. And if you don't have a puppy, it's time to get one, because those guys are adorable. Anyway, you pack your stuff, grab your family, and load up the car. Then you start driving. Soon, the passengers ask, "Where are we going? When will we get there? Are we there yet?" And you realize you don't know. You don't have a map and never really planned the trip to begin with. You're in trouble (and let's be honest, you're pretty terrible at planning vacations—who gave you that job?).

This is what a lot of us do with speaking. We set out with some vague idea of becoming a speaker. We have an idea of what we want to do but don't know much more than that. Where will we speak? What will we speak about? To whom will we be speaking? We aren't sure. Did you know that most successful speakers follow a proven process? They may not know they're doing it, but every professional speaker I've ever met followed the same roadmap. This is good news for us, because if there's a process they followed, we can do the same.

Before we start following that roadmap, we need to start with you. The first step in this journey is deciding you want to be a speaker, that you want to make a difference with your words. That's a declaration you can make to your family, friends, and coworkers today if you want to. If you're afraid of what questions they'll ask, questions you can't answer right away, don't worry. I've got you covered. We'll work through all that. This book will get you on the path to a successful speaking career and help you navigate all those areas you may not have anticipated. I've seen this system work over and over again, so I'm confident it will work for you.

It took me years to figure out the Speaker Success Roadmap, but once I figured it out, everything became clearer. In a way, it made the journey a lot easier because I always knew what I needed to do next. Over the past several years of teaching this system, I've tested and tweaked it with thousands of speakers, and you know what I've learned? It works! Time and time again, the Roadmap is a blueprint for growth and success for any speaker.

If you follow the Roadmap, you'll know where you're going and what to do when you get there. You'll also get bragging rights at the next family party, because you'll be able to answer all the skeptical questions from Aunt Sally and Uncle Sal. And you can finally stop hating Monday mornings.

What Is the Speaker Success Roadmap?

The Speaker Success Roadmap is an easy-to-follow, step-by-step roadmap designed to help speakers start and scale a business from the ground up. It's the tool you need to help you clarify your message, help your speaker brand spread, and create the impact you want to make. It's easy to remember because it's the acronym S.P.E.A.K. Clever, right? Here it is in a nutshell:

SELECT A PROBLEM TO SOLVE.
PREPARE AND DELIVER YOUR TALK.
ESTABLISH YOUR EXPERTISE.
ACQUIRE PAID SPEAKING GIGS.
KNOW WHEN TO SCALE.

Each part of this book will cover a different step in the process. By the end of it, we will have walked through the entire Roadmap together. In each chapter you will get specific action steps and stories to illustrate the process, and at the end of each step we cover, you'll have something practical to do so you can start seeing immediate results. If you follow the steps laid out in this book, you'll be on your way to becoming a successful speaker and living life on your own terms. No more working for someone else, no more dreaming of sharing your story with the world. You can finally stop going around in circles trying to figure it all out. You will be doing it.

Becoming a Speaker

It was 2009, and Erick Rheam had been evaluating his life. As he began to think more about the concept of "lifestyle design," he realized his current job was not giving him the life he wanted. At the time, Erick was working as a customer relations manager at a utility company, which paid well and offered plenty of benefits, but there was something missing. He wanted to have the freedom to do what he wanted, like taking a nap in the middle of the day if he wished, and that just wasn't the case. He felt trapped.

Erick decided to redesign his life and work. First, he left his job and accepted a new position as vice president for business development at a software company, which offered him the freedom to work from home and gave him more flexibility in his schedule. It also allowed him the ability to travel—a personal goal of his.

The following year, while at a conference, Erick had an epiphany. Looking around the exhibition hall, he saw all the other vendors waiting for the next break while the attendees listened to the speaker. At the time Erick had no aspirations of speaking, but as a salesman, he wanted to get in front of the audience.

"How can I separate myself from all these other guys?" he thought. "There's got to be a better way." Then it dawned on him: "I need to be onstage."

After that event, he asked to teach a breakout session at the next conference but was turned down. He kept asking, though, and eventually someone said yes. As Erick started picking up speaking gigs, he discovered how much he loved it. Significance was always something that mattered to him, no matter what he did, and as he spoke, he sensed that this was the *something* missing in his life. He didn't want to be onstage just to represent his company; he had something to say.

By 2014 Erick was speaking regularly but only earning about $5,000 per year in fees. The next year he worked harder, booked more gigs, and made $9,000. He loved inspiring and motivating people, but if he couldn't find a way to make this work as a full-time career, he wouldn't be able to continue devoting so much time to it. He started to feel stuck.

This is not an uncommon story for many speakers. When you're starting out, you need a path to success you can trust. You need to *know* that the steps you're taking are going to lead somewhere significant. You need a roadmap. I met Erick in 2016, and right away he started implementing the steps I outline in the Speaker Success Roadmap. That year, thanks to the Roadmap, he made $30,000 speaking, and the next year he made over $150,000. Today he is a professional speaker, making over $1,000,000 annually in speaking fees (probably more by the time this book is published).

Why did Erick succeed? "I think I'm just an average speaker," he told me. "I just started running through the process and implementing some key things." To succeed as a speaker, you have to be able to deliver a powerful message to an audience, but it takes more than talent to make it in this business. Plenty of skilled communicators can't find a way to make a living off their message. What makes Erick a success is that he had a plan, he worked the plan, and the plan worked. That plan is the Speaker Success Roadmap.

For the rest of this book, I'm going to share with you the system used by Erick, myself, and virtually every other professional speaker I've ever met. If you use it, too, it can change everything.

STEP 1
SELECT A PROBLEM TO SOLVE

Where do we begin? With a problem, of course. Why is this the first step? Because if you don't get this part right, nothing else will work. I think of it as the foundation of a house: the part that isn't flashy and nobody sees, but it is crucial to everything else. When I meet speakers who are struggling, even experienced communicators who aren't gaining traction, I always come back to the same question: "What problem are you solving?" If you don't know that, you can't expect to be booked, because speaking doesn't start with what you want to say. It starts with the problem you want to solve.

The question people most often ask speakers is, "What do you speak about?" It is, of course, the obvious one to ask, but this is the wrong way to think about what a speaker does. We don't just speak on a given topic. We solve problems. That problem could be the problem of boredom or of feeling numb inside. It could be the problem of suffering from a chronic illness or just feeling unmotivated at work. Regardless, your job is to solve someone's problem, not deliver a speech. The speech is the way you get the job done. When people ask you what you speak about, they're really asking, "What problem do you solve? And why should I care?"

No matter how great you are, the audience will always be wondering what's in it for them. Why should they pay attention? What are you helping them with? When we're starting out in our speaking careers, it's not a topic we need to select as much as it's a problem we want to solve. That's step 1 in the Speaker Success Roadmap.

When someone asks what problem you solve, you should be able to answer with the following: *I help <u>GROUP</u> do <u>TOPIC</u> so they can <u>SOLUTION</u>.*

For example: *I help corporate executives maximize their productivity so they can spend more time with their families.*

The main goal is to keep your solution short, clear, and simple. Don't complicate it. My seven-year-old should be able to understand what you mean. If you're clear on the problem you solve, it will be clear to clients whether they should book you. Don't worry about filling in those blanks just yet. Over the next few chapters we'll help you answer each of those questions one at a time. You need to figure out who you're speaking to, what problem you're going to solve, and how you can stand out from everyone else. I call this the "Topic Trifecta" of selecting a problem to solve:

- Choose an **Industry**
- Identify an **Interest**
- Speak with **Integrity**

In the next few chapters, we are going to examine each of these "I" words, and at the end of each chapter, you'll get an action plan with clear takeaways on what to do next. Let's start with Industry, because before you know what you're going to say, you first have to know who you're talking to.

1
Choose an Industry

Melanie Deziel never wanted to be a speaker, but when an opportunity came up at her job, she took it. At the time, she was working for T Brand Studio, a division of the advertising department of the *New York Times*. With both undergrad and graduate degrees in journalism, working there was the culmination of her career, a dream come true. In 2011 the *New York Times* Customer Insight Group published a research study about social sharing, and a tourism conference in Florida requested someone from the company come present the findings. The opportunity worked its way through a number of coworkers, all of whom passed on it, before it landed on Melanie's desk. She was a junior member of the team and thus low on the list of potential speakers, but when no one else took it, she decided to go.

Melanie only had experience speaking to smaller groups, never at a conference or on a stage, but she thought it might be fun. To make matters more complicated, she hadn't written the study, so she was unfamiliar with the content. Now she had to present someone else's research to an audience she knew little about—through a communication format with which she had little experience. She took the opportunity seriously, spending hours reading the report and translating the findings into terms that were relevant to a tourism event in Florida. The talk went well, and she enjoyed it more than expected, which sparked a desire in her to do more speaking.

As fun as the tourism conference was, Melanie realized that if she was going to do more speaking, she would need her own message. She knew she wanted to speak but also knew she needed something of her own to communicate and couldn't just present other people's material. This is true of many speakers. We want to speak but aren't quite sure what we should talk about or what people will want to hear. When we're getting started, most of us are unfocused. We want to speak to everyone and anyone about *all* the things, and that, my friend, just does not work. Melanie began to think about what she was interested in and realized that storytelling, particularly from the perspective of a journalist, was something that fascinated her. But who would be interested in that? She was about to find out.

This brings us to the first step in the Speaker Success Roadmap.

Step 1 is "S," as in "Select a problem to solve." When someone asks you what you speak about, that's not what they really want to know. They want to know why what you talk about is relevant to them. They want to know that you can help them, or someone they know, in some way. In other words, they want you to solve a problem. And that begins with knowing who you're speaking to in the first place.

Know Your Audience

Who do you want to speak to?

This is a question I often ask speakers, and almost always the answer is "I want to speak to everyone, Grant. Everyone needs my help. I want everyone to hear my story. I want to help anyone willing to listen, anyone who needs my motivation, inspiration, and education." That's great. I know it seems smart to cast the net as wide as possible and try to craft a message that appeals to everyone, but it won't work. This is the fastest way to be ignored.

Speaking to "everyone" is really the same as speaking to no one, because who wants to hear a message that's for everyone? It's like buying a coat that's "one size fits all." It's just not true. Either it will be too big or it will be too small, or maybe if you're lucky it'll be just right. It is better to say, "This is who my work is for; it's not for everyone, but it just might be for you." You don't want to speak to all people. You want to speak to the ones who need your message, who are waiting to hear what you have to say, and as soon as they hear it respond, "Yes! This was just for me."

The best way to break out as a speaker is to find an audience who needs your message and speak directly to them. In other words, you have to choose an industry. That's what Melanie Deziel did when she decided to use her experience in the field of journalism to teach marketers how to tell better, more compelling stories. We'll revisit Melanie's story in the next chapter, but for now understand that when she decided to focus on a particular industry, everything changed for her. The same can be true for you.

Make no mistake, though. This is a decision, and like all decisions, choosing what industry you're going to focus on as a speaker will limit your ability to reach other people. In the end, though, it will make you a more effective communicator and a more successful speaker. Why? Because you will be speaking to specific people, and when they hear your message, they'll know it's for them.

So which industry is right for you, and how do you know? Let's look at the most common industries that have a demand for speakers so you have an idea of what to choose from. It may be that you're already in a particular industry and you just didn't know it. Or it may be time to start making some important decisions. Either way, once you focus on an industry, you'll have a lot more clarity concerning who you're speaking to and how to reach them.

Seven Major Industries for Speakers

Knowing who you're speaking to and what that audience expects is crucial to your success. There are seven major industries for speakers that you should be aware of.

Corporations

Large companies are always looking for speakers to help with ongoing training and education, industry events, and company retreats. These companies are a great source of revenue because they tend to have good-sized speaker budgets every year for events. Once you break into this industry, it can create a significant and consistent source of income for you as a speaker. But event planners are typically looking for a certain kind of speaker who fits their agenda, so breaking in can be difficult, and since these events usually pay well, it can be competitive. But once you're in, it can be a very steady source of speaking gigs and clients.

Associations

Associations are any group that gathers around a common cause. The American Psychological Association, Future Farmers of America, the National Press Photographers Association, and the Association for Project Management are all examples of associations. These groups meet around a shared interest or profession and often have large conferences or trainings that are well-funded for speakers. Once you become a part of a certain association's ecosystem, it can be fairly easy to keep getting booked, as many associations have multiple chapters that can refer speakers to each other.

Faith-Based Organizations

Churches, synagogues, and other places of worship are used on a regular basis to gather and have someone deliver a message. This is where I started out speaking, and these venues can be great places to practice and even get paid. Larger religious organizations may have a regular speaking budget set aside for guest speakers, but typically these events don't pay as well as other industries. However, in this industry there tend to be a lot of events, and if nothing else, it can be a great place to practice speaking. Not to mention, if you are delivering a faith-based message, this can be a very meaningful setting to share such a message.

Nonprofits

This includes local groups like Rotary Clubs, chambers of commerce, or other local civic groups, as well as nongovernment and nonprofit organizations that do community work in areas like pregnancy support, job skill training, and health and wellness. This also applies to groups like energy co-ops and credit unions. And don't be fooled by the name; just because the organization is a nonprofit doesn't mean they don't have money to pay a speaker.

Government and Military

This can be local, state, or federal government departments that bring in speakers for events or trainings. The military also brings in speakers for various trainings at their bases as well as other training and support services for soldiers and their families, and the budgets for these events can be quite large. The military is a great industry to break into, because as difficult as it is to break in, once you're in, you're usually in for good. So it can be a place of steady referrals for ongoing work.

Colleges and Universities

Universities are often large entities and hard to get into, so it's better to be more specific and try to speak for groups that gather on campus. For example, this could be new student orientation groups, campus life activities, Greek life (fraternities and sororities), or even student government. Most schools also have hundreds of clubs and student groups on a wide range of topics that may bring in speakers. There are lots of opportunities to speak and get paid for a college gig other than a commencement speech.

Education (K-12)

There are literally thousands of elementary, middle, and high schools around the U.S. Many of them bring in speakers for back-to-school rallies, pretest encouragements, and general assemblies throughout the year. In addition, plenty of schools have opportunities to speak to teachers and parents.

Whenever I share these seven industries, people ask me which one pays the best, which I get, but honestly that's the wrong question. The truth is that speakers thrive in all of these areas if they are good and know how to effectively reach that audience. So the better question is, "Which industry am I best suited for?" And keep in mind, you can't say "all of them." Even if that's true, it just doesn't work. Remember, every potential client wants someone who is just right for their event.

Once you've picked an industry, choosing which problem to solve will become much easier, because now you can narrow it down to a more specific topic. For example, if you're speaking to a group of military leaders, you can now ask the question, "What struggles do these people have, and how can I help?" Knowing who you're speaking to can help you figure out what topic to speak on. So industry comes first, and interest follows.

Which Industry Best Fits You?

If deciding who your audience is right now feels overwhelming, that's totally normal. Choosing an industry is one of the most challenging steps to becoming a professional speaker.

SELECT A PROBLEM TO SOLVE

The worst thing you can do, though, is nothing. Don't assume you have to absolutely know who you're speaking to for the rest of your life. Just pick the industry that seems like the best fit for you right now. Worst-case scenario: you pick the wrong industry, get a few gigs, and have to go back to square one.

That said, here are a couple questions that may help you decide:

- Are you currently working, or have you worked, in one of the seven key industries for speakers? If you have decades of experience in corporate America, breaking into corporate events as a speaker may be easier for you than for others. Do you have connections in a branch of the military that can help you get booked? Pay attention to those kinds of connections. Use what you have, including even the job you may be trying to escape from. Who knows? You may like your industry a lot more if you don't have to work for an employer in it! The idea is to use whatever advantages you have. You're not required to speak in an industry that you've worked in before, but if you have experience that could help your speaking career, you should at least consider using it.
- Which industry do you feel the most passionate about or have the most knowledge in? Of course, experience is not enough. You need to care about this industry. You need to be both knowledgeable and passionate about it, because how else will you be able to relate to your audience? Don't pick an industry just because it pays well or you know you can get

booked. Rather, find a group of people you want to serve, who need your message, and focus on helping them.

Finding the right industry for you is the difference between forcing a square peg into a round hole and fitting your message in just the right place with the right audience. Knowing what to speak about really begins with understanding that your past may be a valuable asset to your future. Just ask Sue Ettinger.

The Veterinarian Whisperer

In 2015 Dr. Sue Ettinger was invited to speak at the largest veterinarian conference in the United States. At that point in her life, she was a busy veterinarian, mother of young children, and like many moms, just trying to keep up with life. Still, she was honored to receive the invitation to speak and took it seriously.

At the conference, Sue delivered six different talks on various subjects, including her core area of expertise: pet cancer. For years she had run a pet cancer awareness program called "See Something, Do Something," and this gig was the perfect opportunity to get the word out on a topic about which she was passionate. After the gig, Sue went home and realized she'd been "bit" by the speaking bug, and she told her husband she needed to figure out how to make speaking more of what she did on a regular basis.

Soon after this experience, though, Sue hit a wall and found it difficult to get more speaking gigs. "I thought it would be easier," she later recalled. Veterinary medicine is its

SELECT A PROBLEM TO SOLVE

own unique world, and she thought she could just meet the conference planners and be "in." But as she says, "There's a game to play." This is always true when working in any industry. There are rules and norms, and if you don't learn them, you're going to pay a big price. So what did Sue do? How did she learn to play the game?

First, she invested in herself, hiring a business coach and taking training programs like Booked and Paid to Speak to learn more about entrepreneurship and speaking. She also read every how-to and advice book she could find on those subjects. Then she started networking, connecting with her industry peers by talking with other veterinary speakers and asking questions about what they had learned.

Early in Sue's journey as a speaker, she would try to connect with as many people as possible and help them. No agenda. No big ask. Just reaching out, talking to people, and trying to solve their problems. Over time, this goodwill spread and eventually came back to her, helping her get plenty of speaking gigs once her professional network knew this was something she was now doing. It was something she had learned in her early years of veterinary practice—the power of a referral—and now she was able to apply the same principle to speaking. For Sue, her most valuable marketing practice is to simply "be a nice person." It turns out that most people want to do business with people they know, like, and trust. Being nice is working out just fine for Sue.

In her first year of speaking, Sue made $35,000. The next year Sue brought in over $70,000, which allowed her to cut back on her veterinary job and speak even more. Today, she is speaking a few times a month and doesn't have to send out cold emails anymore. Most of her speaking opportunities come via referrals from those who have heard her speak before or are in her network. She does do a lot of cancer awareness and education for pet owners through social media, but for conferences and speaking, the audience is predominantly veterinary professionals. She speaks all over the world and has been able to take her family on multiple life-changing, "bucket list" trips to places such as Amsterdam and Maui—all because of speaking.

Sue has built a network of other veterinary speakers and belongs to a number of speaker groups, which have all helped her generate consistent business over the years. She has learned that you have to be patient with the business side of speaking because it's a marathon, not a sprint. Sue studied her industry, did the work, made the right connections, and now she's an in-demand, international speaker in the world of veterinary medicine.

ACTION PLAN

1. List any previous experience or interest you have in any of the seven industries mentioned in this chapter. Try to narrow it down to a few you really like.

2. From there, choose an industry to focus on as you move forward. This isn't permanent. Don't feel like you have to stick with that industry forever. You're allowed to change your mind. But to get started as a speaker, you have to be clear about who it is you want to speak to, so let's just pick something for now.

SELECT A PROBLEM TO SOLVE

3. Choose a secondary industry as a backup in case the first one doesn't end up being what you think it is.

> BONUS: For more help finding the right industry for you, check out our list of resources and tools at SpeakerBook Bonus.com.

Now that we've covered Industry, let's move on to the second area of step 1: Interest.

2

Identify an Interest

What do you want to speak about? What message do you want to share with the world? What are you interested in? These are the questions event planners ask speakers, and it's important you know the answers. Some speakers, however, respond to these questions with their own question: "Well, what do you want me to speak about?" Wrong answer.

Imagine that you walked into a restaurant with no menu to choose from. How would you feel (other than hungry)? Lost? Confused? Maybe even a little overwhelmed? Wouldn't you be a little skeptical of the legitimacy of such an establishment? This is what you're doing as a speaker when you say, "I can speak on anything." As a speaker, you need to narrow your focus by picking a specific area of interest. If I went to a Brazilian steakhouse, I probably wouldn't order seafood. And I wouldn't go to a brain surgeon for a knee replacement. In the same way, event planners want a speaker who will be relevant to their event, and knowing your topic is a way that you can help them make the best decision.

When you go to a restaurant and the server gives you a menu, he is helping you make a decision by limiting your options. But a menu with too many options can be overwhelming, leading you to not decide at all. You may even start to doubt if any of the food is any good. At this point, you're stuck, paralyzed, and you need help making the right decision. Most of us need our options limited so that we can feel in control of the outcome without being overwhelmed by the choices. The same is true for the job of a speaker. You want to limit the options of your client so they aren't overwhelmed, which will help them decide whether you're a good fit. They need you to narrow down your topic to a specific area of interest so they don't have to figure out what it is, exactly, that you speak on. If you don't do this, you're wasting their time and yours, because if a client has to spend time figuring out what your message is, they won't book you or refer you to someone else. Your goal when narrowing down your interest is not to be relevant to everyone; your goal is clarity. If you are clear, others will know whether to book you, and if they realize you're not a good fit, that can still be a win, because they may know someone who does book the kind of speaker you are.

As a speaker, you never want to start with a blank slate (i.e., "I speak on any topic you'd like!"). Set the expectation and own it. You will attract more of the kind of client you want, and you'll fill up your calendar with bookings a lot faster. In the speaking world, there is a temptation to say you do everything for everybody, but in the end it backfires, achieving the opposite of what you want.

IDENTIFY AN INTEREST

For example, say you recently starred on a TV reality show, and now you're a local celebrity. You enjoy speaking but you say, "I'll talk about whatever you want" to a potential event coordinator who wants to book you. They don't want to hear about that. They want to hear about your experience, about the show you were on and what it was like, and maybe the lessons you learned. If they're interested in what you have to share, they'll hire you—not because you speak about everything, but because you speak about something.

How to Narrow Your Interests

You can't talk to everyone. Your message can't be for CEOs, health enthusiasts, entrepreneurs, and married couples all at once. You probably knew that, but most speakers struggle to actually apply this. They get greedy and try to be all things to all people, and it doesn't work. Even if your message is for "everyone," if you try to speak to all those audiences at once, you'll lose them. It's just too broad. You have to focus.

So how do we narrow down our interests to attract more speaking opportunities? Ask yourself the following questions:

1. *What do I enjoy talking about?* Pick a topic you genuinely care about. Are you good at tech, web design, landscaping, and horticulture? Probably not. Even if you have many interests, try to pick one area of interest with an industry around it that hires speakers (don't forget those seven key industries we previously discussed). You're not missing out on an opportunity by narrowing your focus. You're creating one.

SELECT A PROBLEM TO SOLVE

2. *Does it pass the "Five-Year Test"?* Ask yourself, "Can I speak on this topic for the next five years?" If not, pick another topic, because it's going to take time to get known for this area of interest, and you're going to have to be patient.
3. *Are other people interested too?* Just because it's important to you doesn't mean it's important to others. Your topic has to be an interest that solves a real problem people already recognize they have. If not, you're simply sharing a hobby, and that's not enough to book a paid speaking gig.

When you narrow your interest down to a topic other people are interested in, your friends, family, and coworkers will think of you when someone needs help in that area. They'll know how to refer to you instead of saying, "Yeah, I have a friend who likes speaking," which is not helpful. If your closest friends and family aren't clear on what you do, don't expect a stranger to make the connection between what you speak on and the problem they're trying to solve.

Imagine, though, a friend is visiting with a colleague over coffee, and the colleague says to your friend, "I'm hosting an event for singles. Do you know anyone who may be interested in speaking at the event?" And you recently spoke with your friend about this new speaking career you started where you talk to people who are single about finding fulfillment. "Ah, yes," your friend may reply, recalling that conversation in which you were crystal clear on your interest and industry. "I do know someone who speaks about finding fulfillment as a single person. Let me put you in contact." *That's* how this works: you clarify your message, and the clients will come.

If you don't pick a relevant topic, you're going to be in trouble. People can't refer you if they don't know what you're about and what audience you're trying to reach. When you have a powerful topic that others will be interested in hearing you speak on, you are headed in the right direction.

Interest Meets Industry

Remember Melanie Deziel, the *New York Times* employee who spoke at a tourism conference in Florida? Well, that changed everything for her, and Melanie is now speaking all over the world. But things didn't really come together until she identified her interest.

That very first speaking gig was enlightening for her, but she knew it wasn't exactly the kind of speaking she wanted to do. It was on a subject that she wasn't particularly passionate about to an audience whom she didn't know. Through some self-examination, Melanie looked back on what had always interested her, and an area that kept coming to mind was journalism, which she had studied in college. After working for various news outlets over the years, she realized it wasn't just the journalism aspect that excited her. It was the storytelling.

"I had been working as a content strategist for the *New York Times*, Time Inc., and *HuffPost*," she recalled, "where my task was really to use my experience as a journalist to try to teach brands how to think more like journalists, how to tell more authentic stories."

Her recent experience speaking forced her to realize what can happen when you bring together two industries that don't typically talk to each other. In her case, she began to see a need for better, journalism-style storytelling in the marketing world. When you're a marketer, you're used to selling, and storytelling is often an afterthought or a means to an end. But the truth is that the better stories you tell, the better you can sell, and all the basic concepts of journalism apply to the world of marketing. This was both obvious and surprising to Melanie, because nobody seemed to be doing this. She had a unique message to share with a market that needed it.

It wasn't just that she was interested in the topic of storytelling that excited Melanie. That would not have been enough. It was that there was an audience of marketers who were interested in what she had to say. There was a demand for her interest, and that's important, because interest is always a two-way street. You need to be interested enough in your topic to speak on it, but your audience has to want to hear about it as well. If there is no external interest in your topic, you won't be able to book any gigs, and you'll soon be out of a job. If you have to convince people to care about what you care about, then you may be trying too hard. You're better off picking something you know they're already interested in and talking about that. Your best speaking opportunities always lie at the intersection of interest and industry. Your job is to find an established market where people are already getting paid to speak on your topic, and share your message with them.

Shortly after Melanie picked this interest of journalistic storytelling, she was still trying to determine if anyone wanted to hear it. When she received a request to speak at a marketing conference in Denver, she decided to test the waters, saying, "I don't think my company will pay for my

IDENTIFY AN INTEREST

travel. What's your budget for travel and accommodation?" She'd never asked for that before and wanted to see how much they were interested in her and her content. They told her they would cover all her expenses and that they would love for her to speak on authentic storytelling from the perspective of a journalist. She was overjoyed. This was proof that marketers—her ideal audience—were interested in what she was offering—her interest—and they were willing to pay for it.

She landed on marketing corporations and associations as her industry because they were hiring and willing to pay her to speak on a topic she was interested in and passionate about. Plus, she had extensive experience in this field and could speak with excellence about it. She'd found the perfect Topic Trifecta of knowing who she was speaking to, what she was speaking about, and doing so in a way that complemented her strengths. We'll talk more about that third part in the following chapter.

When in Doubt, Watch the Market

But what if you don't know what your passion is? What if you aren't quite sure of your interest or if there's a demand for it? Certainly, it's not as clear for everyone as it was for Melanie. What do you do then? When in doubt, watch the market. Pay attention to what industries are looking for from speakers. What are other speakers in your industry talking about? What problems are they solving?

This was how I got started. As a former youth pastor, I knew that speaking to high schoolers was where I wanted to be. I knew my audience but wasn't sure what to speak to them about. At the time, I had various interests, topics I was passionate about, but that didn't mean there were people willing to pay me to speak about those topics. So what do you do if you aren't quite sure what interest you should pick? This was the challenge I faced early on in my speaking career. It sounds a little crass, but one way to do it is to follow the money. What are event planners already paying for? What does the market demand? Follow the demand, listen to the market, and you'll find paying gigs pretty easily.

As I was starting out, I studied other professional speakers who were doing better than I was. If I met them at an event, I would ask them what topics got the best-paying gigs. I scoured websites of successful speakers and watched their speaker reels to better understand how they were talking about their topics and who their audience was. I was curious what others were getting paid for, and the more research I did, the more I started to see an intersection between what the industry wanted and what I was passionate about.

What that left me with was a focus on leadership for young people, which makes sense considering my background. After my research and connecting with other speakers, I developed two initial talks: "No More Excuses" (about taking ownership and personal responsibility) and "Being a Difference Maker." I had an interest and experience in both and knew that people were hiring for them. But the truth is that it wasn't so obvious for me at first; I was passionate about finance and faith and several other topics, all of which I thought could be "my thing." When I paid attention to what the market wanted, though, the decision was obvious.

You may be interested in many topics. That's great. However, you want to get booked, so listen to what people want,

IDENTIFY AN INTEREST

find the intersection between their demand and your interest, and focus on that. How do you do that? Well, first you need to weed out those who simply aren't interested in what you have to share or aren't worth your time. Ray Edwards, a marketing expert and professional speaker himself, uses what he calls the OPEN method to determine if your audience is interested in your topic. Here's how it works:

> Oblivious: People who don't know they have a problem.
> Pondering: People who are vaguely aware they have a problem.
> Engaged: People who are actively looking for a solution.
> Needing: People whose problem has become overwhelming.*

You want to speak and market yourself only to people who are engaged or needing. Stay away from the pondering and oblivious people. It's hard to convince those people that they have a problem if they don't already know it. So how do you find the engaged and needing people? Nowadays, this is a lot easier than when I launched my speaking business. You can get a really good idea of what the market wants by looking at a few different places:

- *Study other speakers' websites.* Find those who speak in your industry and study their websites. They most likely have their topics listed, and that will give you an idea of what audiences are interested in hearing.

*Ray Edwards, "The Easiest Way to Sell Anything," February 13, 2013, in *Ray Edwards* podcast, https://rayedwards.com/048/.

SELECT A PROBLEM TO SOLVE

Look for people who aren't too far ahead of you to be your guides. It's more helpful to look at people who are about two to three years ahead of you rather than someone who's been speaking professionally for several decades.

- *Study conference websites.* They will have a list of speakers and often the titles or topics of their presentations. Don't just look at the keynote speakers. Check out the titles of breakout sessions and workshops as well. See what themes are the most common.
- *Study speakers' bureau websites.* This is probably a better method for ruling out topics. If you're interested in speaking about something and it's not listed on a speakers' bureau site, go ahead and rule it out, because no one is hiring for it.

Again, the idea here is to not assume what your audience wants. Study what kind of speeches your industry is rewarding, then seek out those gigs specifically. Be careful that you don't spend too much time trying to convince people why they should care about your interest. That's a waste of your energy and time. It's much better to find those who are already interested and find a way to get your message in front of them.

When People Don't Care: The Trojan Horse Method

But what if nobody is interested in the thing I'm passionate about? I hear this question all the time from coaching clients

IDENTIFY AN INTEREST

and podcast listeners. What if you go through the trouble of identifying your industry, picking an interest, and there is just no intersection? Nobody who's interested in your passion? Do you just give up on it? Not necessarily.

When I was first getting started as a speaker, I was speaking at a lot of high schools. Around that time, I was also learning about personal finance and wanted to talk about it to students. However, I had a really difficult time getting schools to hire me to speak on that topic. One hundred percent of school principals would tell me teaching students about personal finance was important to them, but I couldn't find anyone to hire me. What was going on? This is not uncommon, it turns out. You may have an audience who says they care about X, but they still aren't willing to shell out a thousand bucks to have you come present on this topic. What do you do?

That's when you're left with a dilemma. Do you continue to talk about something nobody seems interested in, even if you think it's important? Well, no. That will likely leave you broke and frustrated. So what do you do? Do you give up on your interest and chase what the industry wants? That could make you money, but it'll probably also make you miserable. You'll feel a sense of meaninglessness and eventually resent your job as a speaker. Previously, I mentioned the importance of "following the money" to get an idea of what your market wants, which is a great way to gauge interest. But you don't have to stop there. You don't have to give up on your passions or go broke chasing them.

If you have an interest you want to share but nobody seems interested in paying you to speak about it, you can use what I call the "Trojan Horse Method." Here's how it works. If

SELECT A PROBLEM TO SOLVE

you're having trouble getting booked for a gig around a topic that you know people care about but just aren't willing to pay for, find out what people are getting hired for and position yourself *within* that area. Meaning, start broadly so that you can reach more people but be sure that area includes your passion and interest.

For example, schools weren't hiring me to talk about personal finance, but they were hiring people to speak about transitioning from high school, starting a career, and thinking about their future. Within that subject is the topic of—you guessed it—personal finance. It's a bit broader and more marketable, but once the booking comes in, you can still work in the topics you're interested in talking about. I began speaking to high school students about transitioning to college and adult life, and within that space, I spoke a lot about personal finance. It was fun, and I never received any complaints. Because, remember, principals cared that their students were learning about personal finance; they just weren't willing to book me to speak solely on that topic.

This is the Trojan Horse Method: book yourself for what they request but work in the other topics that you're also interested in. It's not a bait-and-switch, because you're still talking about the main thing, which is like the "horse," but through that vehicle, you're also "smuggling" in another topic that is equally important. It's a sneaky but simple way to work in the topics you're interested in while continuing to get booked and paid to speak. As I said before, opportunity is always found at the intersection of industry and interest. Listen to what people want, but don't forget to give them what they need.

ACTION PLAN

1. Make a list of potential speaking topics you're interested in.

2. Follow the research process in this chapter to identify which of those topics represent speaking opportunities.

3. Decide if you will have to use the Trojan Horse Method to get in front of an audience with one topic and then share another message through that vehicle.

> BONUS: Need help finding a topic that you're passionate about and that your audience will care about? Check out our list of resources and tools at SpeakerBookBonus.com.

Now let's finish step 1, Select a Problem to Solve, with our final area of focus: Integrity.

3

Speak with Integrity

So far in step 1, we've discussed the areas of industry and interest when it comes to selecting a problem to solve. But what if you're saying to yourself, "I'm no expert! I may know something about X, but I don't know everything!" What do you do then?

That's where the third "I" comes in: Integrity.

Lots of people get lost in what I call the "Expert Myth," which is the belief that to say something about a given topic, you have to know everything about it. But is that really true? Will we listen only to doctors who are experts about every area of the body? Do we attend only the concerts of musicians who play every instrument? Do we go only to the restaurants whose chefs can cook every type of cuisine? Of course not. It's the same with speaking. You don't have to know everything to be able to say something.

Being qualified to speak on a given subject means you know more than most on that topic. It does not mean you are the foremost expert on it. If it did, there would be only one person ever who could speak on that topic, and everyone else would be an imposter. All you need to be an expert is to possess some special knowledge or ability that other people don't have. And then you need to be able to share it with them in a helpful way. You don't need to know it all or be able to do it all, but you do need to have integrity.

In other words, you should have the experience and knowledge you say you have. Having integrity doesn't mean doing things perfectly; it just means you are whatever you say you are. It means you follow through on what you said you would do. We're not talking about faking it till you make it or waiting until you reach a special status before you can share your message. We're just talking about being honest about what you can do for an audience and not pretending you can do anything other than that.

For example, my wife, Sheila, and I homeschool our three daughters. Actually, she does 99 percent of it, and I'm just the P.E. teacher trying to flirt with the principal. Anyway, because we've been doing this for years, a lot of people ask Sheila questions about homeschooling. "How did you get started?" they ask. "How does it work? What's a day like? How do you find lesson plans?" These were the same questions we were asking ourselves when we got started. If Sheila wanted, she could speak on this topic at conferences and homeschool conventions—not because she has a degree in homeschooling or because she is a leading authority on the subject, but because she has experience and information others don't have. That's what it takes to be an expert. That's integrity.

Another example: I love the budgeting tool our family uses (YNAB) and recommend it to people all the time. Recently

I posted about it on social media and said, "Hey, this is the software we use for our budget. It's really helped us with our finances." That's all I did. The next day, I received several emails and text messages from friends and family asking if I could help them with their budgeting. By no means am I a finance expert. I just shared a tool that works well for us, and people started asking for advice. Because I know more than they do, to them I am an expert who has something valuable to share. It's the same for you when it comes to speaking on a topic you know better than most.

Now, since the word *expert* is subjective, the challenge here is to position yourself honestly, never claiming more expertise than you really have. When you assume this position of expert, be careful to only share what experience or wisdom you have and don't pretend to be anything other than what you are. When in doubt, remember that you're always the expert of your own story. You can talk about an experience or accomplishment with integrity and expertise, because no one else knows more about what you experienced than you do.

When Opportunity Conflicts with Integrity

Are you what you claim to be? Is your message aligned with your personal experience or interest? Or are you venturing too far from what you know? You don't need to be the foremost expert on a subject, but you do need to have some amount of relative expertise. This can be challenging because the more you speak, the more opportunities will come, and the greater the temptation to step outside your core area of expertise.

My very first paid speaking gig was the Missouri 4-H teen leadership conference. It was for kids with an agricultural background who were interested in farming. Now, let me be clear: I am neither a farmer nor a future farmer. I do not own a single pair of overalls or a straw hat, which I'm pretty sure are prerequisites to be respected by the agricultural community. Anyway, at that event, I didn't know what to expect. Feeling like a fish out of water, I had serious imposter syndrome, thinking to myself, "What am I going to talk with these people about? Why did they hire me?"

However, it occurred to me that I was not stepping onstage to teach these young people new techniques on how to milk a cow. I mean, is that even a thing? I imagine it is. If I had attempted to talk to those kids about farming, that would have been speaking without integrity, because I have no experience or knowledge in that area. But what I could talk about was taking control of your life, which I had experienced in my own life and through my work as a youth minister. In fact, I had seen the same principles illustrated over and over again and was confident in my teaching material. Through speaking to teenagers, I had learned that whether you're a kid in a rural community with a population of two hundred or living in downtown Chicago, you have a lot of the same issues and insecurities. I could speak about that, and I could do so with integrity.

So I stepped onstage that day, in a conference room filled with four hundred teenagers, feeling confident but also thinking, "I hope this works." And it did. After the talk, several kids and adults came up to me to ask if I could speak at their school sometime, and I remember thinking, "If you are terrible, people don't ask you to do it again."

I loved that experience so much I wondered, "What are other events like this?" It turns out Missouri is not the only state with 4-H associations. There are forty-nine others that hold events just like that, so I reached out to the event planner of the Missouri 4-H, asked for a recommendation, and used that to book a gig at a Kentucky 4-H event. I continued this process, sending recommendation letters to all the 4-H chapters I could find. This eventually led to my speaking at nineteen Future Farmers of America events as well. Again, I'm not an agricultural expert, but I speak on what I know, with integrity, and I don't go out of my scope of experience or expertise. People will always pay speakers to do that. That's what integrity is all about: being true to yourself and sharing what you know with people who will listen.

ACTION PLAN

1. Do you know more than most about a topic? Is there something people ask you about? Write down those interests and areas of expertise.

2. Do you have a unique story to tell, something that others relate to? Make a list of anything that comes to mind.

3. Are there certain topics you're unwilling to speak on because they either contradict your values or go beyond the scope of your understanding? Make a list of those boundaries. What will you not speak on, no matter the opportunity? Knowing what you will say

no to is just as important as knowing what you want to say yes to.

As you work through these steps, you will begin to clarify what your interest should be, which is a process of continual refinement, and how to speak on it with integrity.

REVIEW: STEP 1

As we wrap up the first part of the book, it's time to take action on step 1, Select a Problem to Solve. Here's what you should do next:

1. Choose one or two industries you want to focus on per the exercises in chapter 1.

2. Pick a problem you can solve based on your own interest. Don't try to be all things to all people. Focus on what you're passionate about and interested in within your chosen industries.

3. Speak with integrity. You don't have to be the world's greatest expert on a topic, but you need to be confident in your ability to help people and to do so from a place of authority.

At this point, you should now be able to fill in the blanks in this sentence:
I help <u>GROUP</u> do <u>TOPIC</u> so they can <u>SOLUTION</u>.

SELECT A PROBLEM TO SOLVE

The sooner you get this nailed down, the more clear it will become to both yourself and others exactly what you do and don't do, which is the fastest way to start getting booked and paid to speak.

> BONUS: For more help with this step, check out the free tools and resources available at SpeakerBookBonus.com.

Now let's move on to step 2.

STEP 2
PREPARE AND DELIVER YOUR TALK

It may seem out of order to jump right into preparing and delivering your talk before you even have your first speaking gig booked, but this is the next layer in the process. Building a successful speaking career is a lot like constructing a house: you start with the raw materials, laying the groundwork before making it look pretty. So if the first step in the Roadmap—selecting a problem to solve—was the foundation, step 2 is putting up the walls. Now, we're still not painting the walls or decorating the home, but we're getting there.

Before you build a website, make a demo video, or even start emailing anyone to inquire about speaking opportunities, you need to first prepare a talk. Why? Because you have to know *what* you're about before you can put anything on a website or start talking to clients about what you do. Don't rush this step because you're eager to get out there; this is important. The best marketing a speaker can do is not making the right connections or having the slickest promotional material, but simply delivering a great talk.

Let me say that again: the best marketing you will ever do is to give a great speech.

In step 2 we're going to get into what it takes to create an excellent speech and deliver it well. We'll explore six areas in this part, each focusing on a different outcome, beginning with choosing the type of talk and working all the way through polishing and delivering it.

But before we get too far into creating and delivering a talk, we need to discuss the different types of talks to choose from. This decision will likely have the biggest impact on how you go about creating and delivering a message and how successful you are as a speaker. So let's begin.

4

How to Pick the Right Type of Talk

In high school, Dustin Hogan suffered from severe anxiety and depression. "Sometimes just leaving the house felt like climbing Mt. Everest," he said. The anxiety consumed his life and prevented him from doing even the most normal things. When he started college, the anxiety had increased to the point that he would throw up before class. The only relief he experienced was during sleep.

To address the anxiety, Dustin started seeing a therapist, studying personal development, and even experimenting with meditation. During his search for an answer, his constant companion was music. He loved Daft Punk, the Eurythmics, Phil Collins, and U2—anything to lift his spirits. While listening to those bands, he felt an instant connection to the music. He loved dancing and started going to clubs with friends, where he'd notice the DJ and think to himself, "I could do that."

On a whim, he bought an old turntable and began playing with it in his parents' basement. Soon he was working part-time as a DJ. After graduating from college, Dustin worked as a bellman and even had his own landscaping business for a few years before selling the business to pursue music full-time. He moved from Alberta to British Columbia, where he graduated from Stylus College, a music school, and began working as a teacher. Dustin incorporated some of the life lessons he'd learned earlier in life in his daily teaching style, and over time, some of the students sought his advice and counsel, which he eagerly shared. Soon he realized that he had a message to share that extended far beyond music.

Around this time, Dustin joined Toastmasters to help with his presentation skills as a teacher. But the experience did a lot more than that: delivering speeches gave him an exhilaration he had only ever felt while working as a DJ, but with this it went a lot deeper. As a speaker, he was able to share his story and ideas in a manner that moved people in profound ways. He began pursuing speaking opportunities outside of the school.

One of his first gigs was at a student entrepreneurship conference at a local high school, where he did multiple workshops. Although he had done one-off keynote presentations before, he realized they weren't for him. He would much rather go deeper with an audience, even if it was smaller, and focus on helping people experience transformation.

This is a crucial insight and important lesson for any speaker. Keynotes may seem like the exciting thing to do, and they certainly can be, but they're not for everyone. Dustin's desire to see life change in his audience, in part due to his own struggles, meant that more intimate workshops and seminars would be a better venue for his message and work. And that one little insight changed everything.

Eight months later, Dustin launched Rockstar Academy, a seminar designed to teach personal development tools and strategies to people who feel stuck in life. Leading up to this point, he had attended a lot of nearby events, often speaking for free, then wandered around after his talk with a pen and paper, asking for people's email addresses. When he decided to launch that first workshop, he had a small list of email addresses that he'd collected over the previous months from people. He invited all of them to the seminar, and 123 signed up.

To host the event, he rented a small room at a local conference center and set up every chair he could find. His friends came to help but were astounded at his hope, saying, "Dude, we should take some of these chairs down. Do you really think this many people are coming?" This was an honest question, as the event was free, so attendees would have very little invested in attending. But they came, all 123 of them, and when Dustin stepped onstage, he had tears in his eyes. His crazy idea had worked, and this was just the beginning.

At that event, he pitched an in-depth three-day training and sold $3,000 worth of tickets in a single day. He continued to repeat this pattern over and over again—first a free seminar after which he sold a higher-end intensive for those who wanted to take the next step. Today, Dustin runs a successful speaking business, continuing to host one-day seminars where he sells tens of thousands of dollars' worth of training in a single day, and he still DJs on the side.

At his events, Dustin teaches personal development skills he learned earlier in life, and he also has a DJ and encourages the audience to dance during the breaks, incorporating all elements of his story into what he does now. Everything has come full circle, and it's all possible because he isn't trying to be someone he's not. Dustin found the right type of talk for him and built a successful business around doing just that. You will have to do the same—finding which type of talk to focus on will in many ways determine your success. For the rest of this chapter, we're going to explore the three types of talks any speaker can do, the pros and cons to each, and how to decide which one will work best for you.

Keynotes

What is a keynote presentation? A keynote is any speech that captures the main focus of an event. Larger keynotes are often held in convention centers or even stadiums, but a keynote can include giving a talk at your local Rotary Club, a business meeting, or the chamber of commerce.

Keynotes are often shorter than a seminar or workshop, usually ranging from forty-five to sixty minutes long, though they may be shorter or longer depending on the setting. The audience can vary from just a handful of people to several thousand, but the main distinction is that keynotes are one of the primary talks during an event, delivered to the entire audience. For industry events such as conferences, keynote speakers are the ones who typically get paid the most. Depending on your industry, workshop speakers may not get paid as much or at all, but as we saw with Dustin's story, there are other ways to make a living as a seminar or workshop speaker. That said, keynote speakers often make the lion's share of a speaking budget for an event, so if you are looking to make a living as a speaker, positioning yourself as a keynote speaker is not a bad way to go.

Profile of a Keynote Speaker

Since 2016, Jay Acunzo has been delivering keynote speeches. But how he finally realized this was the type of talk he should focus on is another story. While attending Trinity College, he entered and won a sports journalism essay contest. To accept the award, he and his family flew to California, where he gave a thank-you speech to four hundred people, including a handful of professional athletes. A former first baseman for the LA Dodgers happened to be sitting at the same table as Jay's mother, and during the speech, he leaned over to say to her, "Has he done this before? He's a natural!" When Jay's mother shared the story with Jay, he realized he loved speaking and wanted to do more of it.

After college, Jay became a digital media strategist for Google, then worked in the world of venture capital for a while, and spent some time with high-tech start-ups such as Hubspot. Due to the public nature of these jobs, every once in a while he was asked to speak. He recalled that first speech back in college and realized this was what he wanted to be doing full-time. He loved the craft of delivering a keynote. "To me, speaking is not something you do because you have to," he said. "I'm intrinsically motivated by both the performance side—exploring the big idea, feeling the rush of applause or laughter—and the service side—having a real impact . . . and pushing them to create their best work."

Jay's big personality and out-of-the box thinking led to his wanting to help a larger audience, and delivering keynotes was the way to do it. Today, he almost exclusively does keynote speeches. Occasionally, he will do a workshop or breakout session as part of a package, but sharing big ideas with a large audience is what he loves.

What Does a Keynote Speaker Do?

"I'm definitely more of a performer, storyteller kind of speaker," Jay told me, "so I prefer keynotes to practical breakouts or workshops." That is precisely what a keynote speaker is: a performer.

Keynotes are more motivational and inspirational than other types of speeches and therefore require more of the "art" of delivering a great speech. In a sense, it is a kind of performance where you are not just teaching people but encouraging and inspiring—and yes, even entertaining—them. Making people laugh and bringing them on an emotional journey is not a necessary part of delivering a keynote, but having those abilities certainly helps.

Generally, keynotes are broader in scope and intended for a wider audience, so you need to have some piece that keeps them engaged throughout the talk. Often keynotes are delivered in front of a larger crowd whose focal point is you, the speaker, so you want to make sure you are able to hold the audience's attention. Stories are a great way to captivate an audience; whether funny or serious, they keep people engaged and help them remember the message. Other ways to engage people are humor, music, magic, or physical exercises.

Regardless of the group, a keynote always involves some mix of entertainment and core content, whether that's teaching them how to do something or inspiring some sort of change. When I deliver keynotes, I use a lot of humor and stories, keeping the presentation at 75 percent entertainment and 25 percent teaching. For a larger audience, you have to work to keep them entertained and "on your side"; otherwise, you'll lose them. So make no mistake, you're not just there to teach; part of the job is entertaining the audience. As with any group of people, when you're delivering a keynote, you have to earn the right to keep talking to them. Depending on the age and attention span of the audience, you may have to work extra hard. Whenever I speak to high schoolers, I'll tell a seven-minute story to make a two-minute point. That's just part of the job of being a keynote speaker.

Workshops

Workshops or breakout sessions typically range from forty-five to ninety minutes in length. The audience is typically smaller, though often more engaged, than that of a keynote. Depending on the size of the event, you may expect anywhere from twenty-five to a couple hundred people at a workshop. They are usually more intimate and relaxed in nature. Whereas keynotes are more polished and practiced, workshops are a little more loose and interactive.

My approach to workshops is the opposite of how I do keynotes. I like to keep it 25 percent entertainment and 75 percent teaching in a workshop. The audience is there to learn, so they expect deeper, nuts-and-bolts information on a given topic with practical takeaways. Keynotes, by contrast, are broader in scope while workshops tend to be more niche focused. For example, a keynote topic may be "Seven Personal Finance Habits of Successful People," while a workshop at the same conference may be called "How to Set Up a Retirement Fund." Do you see the difference? One is broader and more inspirational, though still helpful, whereas the other is a little more focused.

Workshops appeal to a smaller portion of the audience who really want to go deep with a subject, whereas keynotes stay broad and appeal to a much broader audience. Which is why it's important to know what problem you're solving and who your audience is, because the problem may not be able to be solved with a simple, inspiring keynote. You may need a workshop to do that.

Any time a workshop is part of a larger event, those speakers are not paid very well or at all. So why on earth would you want to be a workshop speaker? A few reasons:

- *To set yourself apart from the competition.* Workshops are a great way to get your foot in the door with conferences and other paying gigs. If your primary focus is on keynotes, this can be a great booking strategy: offer a workshop in addition to a keynote, which will set you apart from another speaker who's only offering the keynote. It can also make you more attractive to decision makers and make you more money.
- *To get more bookings as a keynote speaker.* If I can give a free workshop at a conference, deliver great value, and build rapport with the event planner, there's a good chance they will have me back to

deliver a keynote in the future. I've done this again and again for lots of events over the years. It's a great way to grow as a speaker, become known by your industry, and start working your way onto the main stage, if that's your goal. So just because you might not consider yourself a "workshop speaker" doesn't mean you should completely avoid them.

- *To get a free ticket to a conference you want to attend.* I've used this method a few times to get into a conference for free. Several years ago I offered to teach a workshop at a conference that cost $1,000 per ticket, and they gave me free registration for teaching. That was a win for me, because I would have paid to attend. They didn't pay me, but I got $1,000 in value from offering to speak for free. Plus, you never know what that kind of exposure may lead to.
- *To test new speaking material.* Workshops are a great way to learn about an audience and try new things to get real-time feedback. Normally I would never try new, untested speaking material in a high-pressure keynote with a few hundred or a thousand people in the audience. In a situation like that there's no room for error, and if you make a mistake, it's a lot harder to recover. Workshops, on the other hand, are more casual and less intimidating, so they can be a much better place to try out new content. There are fewer people, and the talk doesn't have to be as scripted, so it provides a fantastic opportunity to see how people respond to your new story, joke, or idea. If it works, great! Put it in a keynote or future

workshop. If not, no big deal, and you haven't embarrassed yourself on a big stage.

- *To experiment with content you want to use elsewhere.* Seeing how people react in person will give you an idea of whether it is effective in other formats. Most of the content in this book has been tested first through live workshops and then through online courses. Never underestimate the importance of understanding your audience and getting live feedback. Delivering a message or teaching in person, while reading their faces and body language, will give you a much better idea of what they think than simply reading a survey. Not to mention, if you take questions from the audience, you can understand where they're coming from and how you can help them. There's nothing quite like delivering content live, so try to take advantage of such opportunities when you can, because it can be converted into other, even nonspeaking, material later.

Profile of a Workshop Speaker

In 2009 Robert Rose left his job as the chief marketing officer of a software company and started his own consulting business. Starting out, he found that speaking was one of the best ways to get new leads, so he took every speaking gig he could take, free or paid—it didn't matter. Those first few gigs came from tapping all the personal and professional connections he had, and like many successful speakers will tell you, he discovered that the biggest means of lead generation for speaking is more speaking.

After Robert had honed his speaking chops some more, he started to focus his message and determine who his ideal audience was, realizing workshops were his real bread and butter. Now he speaks to audiences around the world about content creation and storytelling in marketing, two topics he is passionate about and qualified to speak on.

Robert does both keynotes and workshops. Unlike some speakers who focus on keynotes as their primary source of revenue, though, he sees keynotes as lead generation for the daylong, boot-camp-style workshops he does. He does between thirty and thirty-five keynotes per year, twenty of which are paid, and the rest are free but lead to other opportunities.

"Keynotes," he said, "are a means to an end. A profitable means to an end, but a way for me to secure other work. I think of keynotes like pop songs. They're self-contained performances. But workshops are learning and curriculum based. They're meant to have a certain outcome, which truly enables people to do something they couldn't do before." If you are an educator who finds that kind of transformation rewarding, as Robert does, workshops may be the type of talk you want to focus on.

Seminars

Seminars and trainings can last anywhere from a few hours to a few days and allow you to go deeper on a given topic. Typically, speakers who offer these types of in-depth trainings are hired by companies to help with a specific topic. But you can also do your own trainings, like Dustin Hogan does, if you have built a large enough audience interested in hearing from you.

With these types of talks, you are often working with larger, corporate audiences, where companies hire speakers to come do a training for a certain department or sometimes a company-wide team-building day. If you choose to focus on seminars, you will want to have many interactions and activities planned for this setting instead of just you talking. If you're presenting multiple days' worth of material, it's going to be very difficult for you to talk that long and keep the audience engaged. Having planned discussions and small-group work will help break up the presentation for the audience, making it more practical and dynamic. This can also make a big difference in how much they learn and take away from your teaching.

Profile of a Seminar Speaker

Dave Delaney was first exposed to speaking in Ireland when he started performing improvisational comedy. In Galway, he was asked to teach an improv workshop at a business, which went so well that it sparked an idea to lead corporate communication workshops using what he learned from comedy as the basis for the teaching, which he still does today.

In his seminar Dave teaches participants to use the rules of improv, combined with additional communication training, to stop fearing failure, become empathetic, and learn to listen. He gets a lot of laughs too. "With smaller, more intimate groups," he said, "I am able to address specific challenges they may have to ensure they are completely satisfied with my training. One of my goals is to bring teams together to connect and learn from one another. It's wonderful to see the shyest introverts interact with the most outgoing extroverts in a cohesive way."

HOW TO PICK THE RIGHT TYPE OF TALK

Dave is another example of a speaker who uses keynotes and large conferences as lead generation tools for his seminars. If you're interested in doing seminars, there are seminar companies that will hire and train you. These companies include Skillpath Seminars, National Seminars, Fred Pryor Seminars, and others. Though they find bookings for you, you're still an independent contractor and are free to book your own gigs. Typically these companies don't pay you very much and the work can be pretty grueling, but the experience is invaluable and a great way to break into the seminar space. When I did this kind of work early on in my speaking career, I once did five cities in five days, didn't get paid much for my work, but it was great practice and led to other opportunities to speak.

Which Type Is Right for You?

How do you know which type of talk is right for you? The best way to know is through trial and error. Try doing one of each and see which you enjoy the most. Before you do that, however, it would help to do your research to see what these types of talks look like in the real world.

To find examples of different types of talks, I would start online. For keynotes, TED Talks are great, as they often showcase great speakers and are short, so you can watch a lot of them in a small amount of time. YouTube can also be a good place to hunt for great talks, such as commencement speeches and the like.

For workshops and seminars, you'll probably need to attend local conferences and events and see them in person. Of course, you can pay to attend these events, but that can also end up being quite expensive. Another way is to offer to work as a volunteer for the event and receive complimentary admission, which is quite common. While working the conference, try sitting in on a keynote, then go to a workshop and see how they compare.

Learn from the examples of others, and you'll get a clear idea of what type of talk resonates with your style of communication. And of course, you always have the option to offer all three types of talks to speaking clients. You just need to have a clear strategy for why you're doing this and the purpose of each type of talk.

Creating Your Menu

Remember our restaurant analogy? If a waiter were to say to you, "Oh, we can just cook whatever you want," you'd probably not be able to think of anything. We may think that if this restaurant can cook anything, they probably don't cook it very well. People like options. It gives them a sense of peace and confidence in their choices. That's what creating a speaking "menu" is all about.

A speaking menu is a list of options available to your client, including what types of talks you do, what topics you cover, and the ideal audience for each type of presentation. The easiest way to get started is to begin with what you want to talk about and what kind of presentations you want to do. If you have no idea, try identifying your audience to understand what topics get booked and what those clients need. As you get more experienced and learn about what works and what you like, your menu will evolve and change. Like a good restaurant owner, try to keep your options limited

HOW TO PICK THE RIGHT TYPE OF TALK

while still considering what kind of choices your audience prefers. In my own speaking, I offer keynotes on two different topics and workshops with four different topics. That's my menu. It's simple and effective, which is the goal.

ACTION PLAN

1. Choose what type of talk you're going to focus on: keynotes, workshops, or seminars. You may do a variety of them, but where are you going to focus your attention and energy, at least initially?

2. Create a menu of talks that clients can choose from. Focus on a few offerings that appeal to different audience segments for your target industry.

3. Build a plan for finding more gigs for the kind of talk you want to do. Research events in your industry that are well attended and booking other speakers for those types of talks.

> BONUS: To see examples of speaking menus and other resources, visit SpeakerBookBonus.com.

5

How to Create a Great Talk

Now that we've explored the three different types of talks, it's time to create one. Before you start scripting your message, though, you need to know what you're trying to do. What's the goal? What do you want to accomplish with your message? As a speaker, you should always have a clear objective, and until you are clear on that, everything else is going to feel like a waste of time.

When you're watching a movie and start to feel lost, you think to yourself, "What is the point of this?" Don't do that to your audience. When you're clear on where you're taking them, the preparation process becomes much simpler. Which makes sense, right? When you know where you're headed, it's easier to create a map for how to get there. Your job as a speaker is to bring your audience along with you for the ride, and to do that well, they need to start at the same place and arrive at the same destination as you do. The goal in preparing a speech is to become clear on your destination so that everything in your talk points to that one insight, principle, or application. You never want to leave the audience wondering, "What was the point of that talk?"

A good talk should always answer two questions:

> Question 1: "So what?" What is the one thing you want your audience to know by the end of your speech? You never want them to feel confused about the message you were trying to get across.
>
> Question 2: "Now what?" What do you want them to do about it? What's the next step? Where do they go from here?

Answering "So what?" and "Now what?" is your first job as a communicator. That's your objective. Before you begin practicing your speech, you must be clear on the answers to those two questions. As you develop your speech, consider these questions with each step of the journey. They will help you stay focused and clear.

But what if there are several things you want your audience to know? That's a natural question, but going in too many different directions will likely confuse the audience, so be careful. As you consider the many things you want to say in a talk, try focusing on the most important point you want to make and save the rest for future talks. As you develop a menu of speeches, there's a good chance you'll have opportunities to use most of your ideas in future talks. The process is always one of pruning. A general rule is that the more you cut, the better the talk is going to be.

Determining your objective is a discovery process and will likely evolve during the preparation period and even after you deliver the talk a few times. Over time, the focus may shift, and the talk itself will keep getting stronger as you figure out exactly what you want to say and how to say it. So how do you know what objective to start with? At first you're just giving it your best guess, but after you speak a few times, you'll get more feedback and a clearer idea of what you're trying to do. Your talk and its objective will get better and sharper over time, but we all have to start with where we are.

Reducing your talk to a single, powerful idea will allow you to create an entire talk around the one thing you most want to communicate. Having one big idea makes it easier for people to follow your presentation, which translates to a more enjoyable and more memorable experience for the audience.

Four Ways to Structure Your Talk

In his book *Steal the Show*, Michael Port discusses several frameworks for a speech, and I would like to include four of them here: numerical, chronological, modular, and problem-solution.*

The *numerical* framework is most commonly used and involves structuring your talk around a certain number of principles, such as the "7 Habits of Highly Effective People." Generally, odd numbers tend to work better because they catch people's attention and offer a clear promise for what the audience is going to get out of the talk. With this type

---

*Michael Port, *Steal the Show: From Speeches to Job Interviews to Deal-Closing Pitches, How to Guarantee a Standing Ovation for All the Performances in Your Life* (New York: Houghton Mifflin Harcourt, 2015).

of talk structure, less is more. The fewer points you have, the more likely your audience will remember them and the stronger each point will be. I recommend having three to five points in a speech, as more can be overwhelming. A great speech is as much about what the speaker decides to leave out of the speech as it is about what they choose to include. These points can be referred to as keys, principles, ideas, rules, or concepts, and they all need to point back to the main objective.

In the *chronological* framework, each step builds on the previous one, like laying brick on brick for the foundation of a building. This structure can be easy to memorize because the steps have to go in a certain sequence or they won't make sense, which also makes it easy for the audience to remember what you said. For example, I have a "Life Is a Highway" presentation that covers three points: past, present, and future. It's a motivational talk for college students on how life is an adventure, and the sequential structure works because each point builds on the previous one. I know exactly where I'm going, as does my audience. This type of talk can create a sense of momentum that keeps building and building until you reach the final point.

The next framework is *modular*, which allows you to go in order, but it's not necessary. With this structure, you are also free to skip around. If you forget a point, you can always go back to it later or even play with rearranging the order depending on the audience. My online course The Art of Speaking, which is a lot like an online seminar for speakers, is set up this way. The course makes sense if you follow each module in the order in which it's taught, but every section stands alone as a unique teaching unit and doesn't necessarily need the preceding information. With this structure, you can bounce around within the message and it still makes sense. It's more of a choose-your-own-adventure type of speech, and because of that, it can be fun to give over and over, tweaking the order each time.

The last type of framework is *problem-solution*. This is where, obviously, you present a problem and offer a solution. With this type of talk, you can have one big problem that you're trying to solve, or you can have a series of problems and solutions that go in some kind of order, in which case your problem-and-solution would make up a single point in the talk. Again, you don't want to exceed more than a handful of points in a single talk, but you want to offer many problems and solutions until you achieve your objective. For example, if you need help finding and booking speaking gigs, I can offer a solution to that. Need help making sales? There's a solution for that. And on and on you go until you've helped your audience achieve a solution to whatever the main problem is they're trying to solve. That's problem-solution.

Finding a Rhythm for Your Talk

Once you know your talk structure, how do you organize it? Before we get into outlining a talk, you need to figure out a way to make it flow. The rhythm I use in my speeches is this:

1. Present a point.
2. Expand on the point.
3. Tell a story to illustrate the point.

4. Help the audience apply the point. This is where the "So what?" and "Now what?" come in.
5. Repeat.

In addition to an introduction and conclusion, this is all you need to organize an effective talk. I use this rhythm in all of my talks and repeat it over and over, and it's very effective.

That said, there's no "right" way to create a talk other than what seems natural to you and works with the audience, so feel free to try out different formats and ways to make the talk flow. Find a process that works for you and the audience. Don't get married to your manuscript too early on. Prepare your speech but allow for spontaneity and improvisation; trying out new things and experimentation are part of the process to create a great talk.

Using Stories in Your Speeches

Stories are one of the most powerful tools in a speaker's toolbox, and learning to use them well is an essential skill for becoming a successful speaker. Why are stories so powerful?

- *Stories engage people's attention.* As soon as you say, "Let me tell you a story," people's ears perk up and they immediately focus on what you're saying. If I'm losing an audience in the middle of a speech and begin to tell a story, I know I'll get them back. Once we start listening to a story, it's difficult to stop. We want to know how it ends. Using stories to engage an audience is an effective way to lead them through your talk, especially during the parts when they may otherwise disengage or get distracted.

- *Stories are memorable.* If you were to ask someone what they remember from a speech they heard a week ago, they probably wouldn't be able to cite the statistics they heard or that wonderfully eloquent quote the speaker memorized; they may not even remember the practical application the speech had in their lives. But they most certainly will remember the stories the speaker told. As human beings, we are naturally wired to understand our lives narratively, as we constantly use stories to help us make sense of the world around us. So telling a good story is a great way to make your points stick.

- *Stories make it easier for the presenter to remember the points in the presentation.* If you have pages and pages of technical information that you want to communicate, it will be difficult to remember and even harder to present. Stories are easier for you to remember and can trigger in your mind the point you wanted to make. They're a great bridge between points and a wonderful way to entertain an audience.

How to Capture Stories

A few years ago I took a trip to Walt Disney World with my family. My daughters dressed up as princesses, and the cast members kept addressing them as "princess" all day long. At the end of the day, my oldest daughter said, "Daddy, I think they really believe I'm a princess." When we got back to our car, I immediately wrote that down. I wasn't sure how, but I knew that someday I would work that story into a talk. It's important to get into the habit of capturing stories.

Be on the lookout for good stories, and develop a process for remembering them. Come up with a system for capturing them, whether it's a piece of software, your smartphone, or a notebook. If you are not already in the habit of doing this, please start, because when you hear a great story, you think you'll remember it, but believe me, you won't. Always have your "radar up," so to speak, so that you're aware of the stories when they come, because you just never know when you might stumble across a good one. Pay close attention to what's going on in your life and around you and write down anything that you think might be good for a future talk.

In addition to capturing stories, take an inventory of all the great stories you already have. When you do this, focus on the incident itself, not the meaning or application. Sometimes speakers get hung up on figuring out what the point of a story is or why they would even tell it, but that's not where you should begin. With the Disney princess story, I didn't know what I would do with that story; I just knew that it felt significant when it happened. At this point, all you're trying to do is answer the question, "What happened?" We'll come back to the practical part later.

Often, though not always, first-person stories, the ones you actually lived, are the most powerful because you can tell them in an emotionally compelling way, recalling details and feelings that make it feel real to the audience. Certainly, you can also tell stories or anecdotes from other people's lives or perhaps from a book you read, but the ones you have personally experienced, because they are more relatable, will usually bring a greater connection to the audience. They're also more important to you, and the audience can feel that in the passion and strength of your delivery.

Coming Up with Story Ideas

In *Steal the Show*, Michael Port mentions a quick and easy way to brainstorm story ideas from your own life:

- Think about people: your first boss, your high school sweetheart, a coworker, one of your kids, your spouse, your crazy cousin Eddie.
- Think about places: your first job, your favorite vacation spot, your best friend's house, the first place you lived on your own, your college dorm room.
- Think about things: your first car, your high school yearbook, your favorite toy, a trophy, a medal, a painting or picture that has meaning; just take a look at stuff around your house.
- Think about events: a time when you got in trouble, your first day of school, the day your child was born, the day you got married, a moment when you got bad news, an accomplishment; go through old Facebook pictures to trigger memories.[*]

Is something, anything, coming to mind? Write it down. Don't judge it or worry if it's good enough; just get a list going.

By now you may have some good ideas for stories you want to tell and just need to put the pieces together. The

---
[*]Port, *Steal the Show*, 107–8.

next step is to write out the story, even if you've lived it. For example, I could tell you off the top of my head how I got engaged to my wife, but if I stopped to think about it, I could come up with more details that would make the story even better. You could probably do the same with plenty of stories from your life; when you take time to write out the details, you may realize there are all kinds of interesting things you'd forgotten.

Eventually you'll have a list of stories, and you've taken the time to write them out. Now it's time to filter them for your talk. Which stories should you use for your speech, and how should you use them?

- *Share stories that contribute to your main idea.* Remember, the details don't need to relate exactly to your main idea, but the application must. For example, I could tell the story of my first car to a group of high schoolers or a group of entrepreneurs. I'm not telling that story only to car enthusiasts, because I can make it apply to many audiences and settings. For this reason, you want to share stories that can have many broad applications depending on the speech and audience.
- *Only share details that move the story forward and are critical to understanding it.* For example, let's look again at the story of getting engaged to my wife. I got engaged June 27, 2001, in Springfield, Missouri; it was a Thursday. I proposed in a park, and if you drive down National Avenue heading north you'll see it on your right, right behind Cox Hospital. Bored yet? An audience certainly would be. These

details distract the listener and do not have anything to do with getting engaged. Maybe an audience in Springfield, Missouri, would be interested in these details, but no one else. In another story about losing my wedding ring on a canoe trip, the color of the canoe doesn't matter. What river it was also doesn't matter. If the detail doesn't move the story forward or help anyone understand the application, drop it.

- *When filtering stories, be aware of the emotion you want your audience to have.* A good question to ask yourself is, "What do I want my audience to feel when I share this story?" That will help you know how to tell the story. Stories can be funny, inspirational, sad, or thought-provoking. They can encompass one or two of these emotions or all of them at once. There are times when I tell a story and it is sad and thought-provoking, so I throw in a funny line just to break up the tension, because I want to leave my audience feeling entertained.
- *Stories can vary in length.* Sometimes you can tell a story in thirty seconds, and that's all you need to get the point across. Others may be longer. I tell certain stories that are six or seven minutes long, because that's how long they need to be to get the point across. Your talk may center on your entire life story, so the whole speech could be one long story jumping in and out from scene to scene. That's fine, so long as the length of the story supports the points you are trying to make and it doesn't last one second longer than needed.

- *Pay close attention to the transitions from your stories back to the point you are trying to illustrate.* Again, it all comes back to "So what?" and "Now what?" Always keep in mind that the audience will be wondering why you just told them that story. Make sure you have a smooth transition into the application or next part of the talk so you don't leave listeners wondering what that was all about.

Using Humor in Your Talks

Humor is extremely effective for keeping an audience engaged. Think about stand-up comedians, who are usually very effective public speakers because they are used to standing in front of people for long periods of time and keeping them engaged. When using humor as a speaker, you're earning an audience's trust, letting them relax, and getting them on your side.

That said, you don't have to be a comedian to use humor in a talk. The challenge of being funny sometimes intimidates or holds speakers back, but the truth is, anyone can use humor in a speech, even in ways that don't involve telling jokes. For example, you could tell a funny story, come up with a few clever one-liners, or even share a humorous picture or video that does the work for you. You don't always have to write or come up with some hilarious joke. You could simply share a funny meme or quote in your presentation. The point is that when you get an audience to laugh, you will win them over.

One of the easiest ways to lighten a talk is by using self-deprecating humor. It's easy and safe to make fun of yourself rather than someone else. Just remember, as with stories, humor should be used within the context of "So what?" and "Now what?" Don't tell a joke just for the sake of being funny. It should move the point of the talk or story forward; it should prove your point somehow. A lot of comedy is situational—paying attention to the things around you. Many comedians start with the line: "Have you ever noticed . . . ?" Again, this comes down to keeping your radar up at all times and taking notice of things that strike you. Watch comedians. What do they find funny? What does the audience laugh at? Use those things as clues to help you figure out how you can use humor in your own presentations.

Another good place to find humor for a talk is social media. Look for something that is getting a good reaction, lots of likes and shares, and see if you can use it in your presentation. If it works on social media, it will probably work in a speech. A word of caution, though: never steal from others. Don't tell stories that are not your own. If you do this, word gets around quickly, and you'll eventually get caught. I've heard of plenty of people who stole material and eventually lost work as a result. You don't want that kind of reputation. If you do use a story that isn't your own, be sure you give credit to the original source.

Here are some additional tips for using humor:

- *Take an unexpected detour.* Years ago, there was a big health scare on the news, and I was giving a presentation at the same time, so I opened with, "Hey, here's an important thing I want you to catch—not Ebola." It was funny because it was relevant to that time and took an unexpected turn. They thought I was going *here*, and instead I went *there*, and everyone burst out laughing.

- *Pay attention to context.* One time I was speaking in a hotel that was also hosting the president of China. It was a big summit with many world leaders, and there were Secret Service agents and Chinese media swarming everywhere. So I opened my talk by making a list of things not to do when sharing a hotel with the president of China. Of course, this only worked within this specific context. If I had gone to Kentucky and opened with that, people would have been confused. It was the shared context that made it funny.
- *Some of your best jokes may come off the cuff.* This happens to me sometimes when I'm onstage and get an idea or feel a little brave, so I say something unplanned. Sometimes it works, sometimes it doesn't. But often that "in the moment" inspiration is just right and you'll discover a great joke you can use again. Don't be afraid to trust your intuition when those ideas come.
- *Never tell the audience, "This will be funny."* It's always too much pressure and sets you up for failure because the bar is too high in the audience's mind. The best jokes sneak up on people.
- *Don't forget timing.* If you rush through a joke, it won't be funny.
- *Allow the audience a chance to laugh.* Pause so they don't miss the next thing. If you keep moving too fast

and talk through their laughter, they won't hear the next joke or point you want to make.
- *Always be appropriate.* Be careful not to tick off the decision maker. If you've made everyone else laugh but you've offended the event planner, that's not a win. You never want to cross a line with the client that results in your not being invited back.
- *Take notes.* When you get offstage, write down your punchlines and how well they worked this time, especially if it was your first time trying out a joke. Humor is a skill that takes time to develop, and those who practice it the most win.

So let's say you have some jokes you'd like to try. Start by testing humor in low-pressure settings, which means you don't try out a new joke at the biggest event of your life. If you do workshops, those are great places to try new material. Just like stories, jokes and humor evolve over time, but you never know if something will work until you actually get onstage and try it. When writing your talk, you may think what you're writing is funny, but you never know until you test it out on real people.

If a joke doesn't work, move on. Don't explain it. There are going to be times when a joke falls flat, and that's okay. Just keep going. Trying to explain it never works and will make it more awkward for the audience. Sometimes, when a joke doesn't work, I may even make a little joke of the joke, saying, "Okay, mental note: that didn't work, don't use that joke again," and often that will actually get a little laugh. It's okay to poke fun at yourself and use that self-deprecating humor I mentioned earlier. Just don't linger too long if something you said wasn't funny. Keep the speech moving.

Of course, the audience has a part to play here as well. Some jokes will land better than others depending on the environment. We're going to talk later about how your setting can affect a presentation, but for now, know that sometimes you can tell a joke in a certain space and it works great, then you tell it again and it falls flat. It's not always you; the audience can affect how well a joke works. Keep working with the joke, and you'll see when and where it works best. Humor can be hard, but it's an invaluable tool for a speaker.

Writing Out Your Speech

Once you're clear on what the speech is about and what kind of talk it is, it's time to write the whole thing out. Here's how I recommend doing that:

1. *Brainstorm the topic and make a list of bullet points.* These can be stories, points, stats, etc. Do not filter your ideas right now; you'll organize later. At this point, you're just getting everything down on paper. You can handwrite this, mind map it, use a tool like Evernote or Word, put ideas on sticky notes, or even audio record yourself. The important thing is to have no filter at all and just get it all out.
2. *Organize those ideas into an outline.* What are the main points that stand out to you? What are the supporting details that work well for each main point? Look for stories and anecdotes that relate to the points.

3. *Expand your outline into a manuscript.* This is where you add meat to the bones by fleshing out your stories and points. Write out your transitions. As you're developing all this, don't be married to your structure. Be willing to make changes as the talk evolves. You might start out designing your talk with a numerical structure and realize that it makes more sense to use a modular structure. That's totally fine. Sometimes you only find out these things by workshopping. Even as you deliver the presentation you will probably realize you need to change things if something doesn't seem to click with the audience the way you want it to. A talk is always a work in progress.

ACTION PLAN

1. Get clear on the main idea for your speech.

2. Identify what stories or jokes you're going to tell.

3. Outline it.

> BONUS: Additional resources on the art of public speaking can be found at SpeakerBookBonus.com.

6

What to Do before You Step Onstage

Mark Twain once wrote, "There are two types of speakers: those that are nervous, and those that are liars." Even Elvis said, "I've never gotten over stage fright. I still go through it every show." If great orators and famous performers get nervous, chances are you and I will too. Public speaking is the number one fear for most people, more terrifying than heights, death, flying, loneliness, bugs, or snakes. And why is that? I think it comes down to three unspoken fears:

- *Fear of the unknown.* When we step onstage, we don't know how it's going to go. The experience of speaking before a live audience could be phenomenal, or it could be a disaster. And that feeling of uncertainty naturally creates anxiety.

- *Fear of embarrassment.* What if I say something stupid? What if people laugh when I'm not telling a joke? What if no one laughs when I am telling a joke? What if people aren't paying attention? What if they say mean things about me afterward? What if, what if, what if? It takes a lot of courage to face the scorn and even disapproval of your peers, and each time you give a speech, that's certainly a possibility.
- *Fear of the worst-case scenario.* Whatever that looks like to you: maybe the audience hates you, or they throw things at you, or you never get booked again. All of these are unlikely, but this is the definition of a worst-case scenario: something terrible that could potentially happen. We fear bad things happening even though we understand they probably won't. Nonetheless, the fear is there.

So what do we do with these fears that prohibit us from speaking or that can even affect our performance onstage? First, acknowledge that all good things in life come with the possibility of failure. Anything you try—whether it's giving a speech, starting a business, launching a podcast, or writing a book—can, and sometimes does, fail. In fact, many new and exciting projects crash and burn the first few times, but that shouldn't stop you from attempting great things.

Second, remember that fear is not always bad. There are two things it can do for you: (1) fear focuses your attention; (2) fears tells you something is important. The fear reminds us that this work matters; if it didn't, we wouldn't care.

WHAT TO DO BEFORE YOU STEP ONSTAGE

Think about when you're getting ready to ask someone on a date or hit publish on that new blog post or apply for a job. Feeling nervous means you care, and certainly, that's true for public speaking. If you aren't at least a little nervous about an upcoming gig, which I honestly feel every time I get ready to speak, then that may mean you're not taking it seriously enough. Fear, at times, can be a good thing, a reminder to us of what's really important.

Finally, understand that excitement is often misinterpreted as fear. The body's reactions to fear and excitement are almost identical, which means that the way to face the things we're afraid of can be as simple as making a decision. The next time you feel afraid, ask yourself, "Am I afraid of this or just excited?" For example, some people are scared to death of roller coasters, and others absolutely love them. If you're someone who loves roller coasters, you probably still feel butterflies each time you get on the ride, no matter how many times you've ridden. Are you actually scared? Probably not. You just can't wait for the thrill of what's to come.

Every time I get ready to step onstage, I remind myself that I love this work, that I chose to do this, and I'm not actually afraid of what's going to happen—I'm excited. The more I tell myself this, the more I feel it; and though the butterflies don't go away, I know that speaking is something I'm supposed to do. Fear causes you to flee from the thing causing it, whereas excitement causes you to run toward it.

That said, there are a few things we can do to manage the discomfort of speaking in front of an audience and make sure we are ready to step onstage and do our best work.

Practice Makes Peaceful

One of the best ways to calm your nerves as a speaker is to practice your talk over and over again. Showing up prepared gives you confidence that cannot be faked. There is a significant difference between the nerves that come with excitement and the ones that come with feeling like you're not ready. If you're being honest, you can usually tell when you haven't prepared enough. You can feel it.

Imagine you're back in school. You walk into class and the teacher starts passing out a test. How do you feel? If you didn't study, you're probably a mess. You may feel anxious or nervous or even expect it not to go well. But if you studied, you feel fine. If you've done practice tests and put in the effort, you feel confident and comfortable and ready to do this. It's still a test, of course, so you may still feel nervous, but if you've prepared, you are going to feel markedly better than if you didn't. That's what rehearsing a talk can do for your delivery.

Practicing your talk may not sound exciting, but it can make a world of difference in how you feel when stepping onstage. What makes a speaker great is the work we often don't see—the hours he or she has put into the talk before ever delivering it. Sometimes, it may seem as though certain speakers just get up there and wing it, but I can assure you this is almost never the case. If you assume that this is what you can do as a professional, you will almost certainly fail. Professionals practice, and if you want to succeed as a speaker, you will have to do the same.

The mark of any professional is practice. Even though athletes put in thousands of hours playing the game, they still practice every week, sometimes even daily. Practice is what makes a speaker not just good but great. Great speakers put in the work when no one is watching, so when it's time to perform, they're ready for whatever comes their way. Diligent practice is what will make you look like a natural, whereas winging it will always leave you seeming scattered, unorganized, and amateurish.

Practicing also helps you to be more present to your audience. Some speakers are trapped in their own mind, thinking of what they're going to say next, because they didn't practice. The more you go over the talk, the more comfortable you will feel, and the more you can be fully in the moment with the audience. They will feel this presence, even if they can't understand why, and as a result, they will trust you more. I'd like to remind you that when you're speaking, you don't get a second chance. You don't get to try a story over again or redo it in a different order. When you're up there, you get one shot, and being fully present will help you get it right the first time.

How to Rehearse a Talk

Let's go back to where we left off in the last chapter. By now, you should have your entire talk outlined and written out as a manuscript. To get more comfortable and confident with the talk, the next step is to read the entire speech out loud. At this point, you may have worked on different parts at different times or out of order. Maybe you've even added different jokes or stories to the speech, or maybe this is the first time you're looking at it. Regardless, you now need to read it through as one continuous piece.

As you do this, ask yourself the following questions:

- How does it flow?
- Does it make sense in this order?
- Is there a logical sequence?
- Are the transitions smooth?
- Does the story transition nicely into the point?
- Is anything confusing?
- Is your one objective clear, the one key idea you want people to leave with?
- Do the stories support the objective of the talk?

While you do your read-throughs, focus on the content more than on how you'll present it—we'll cover delivery in chapter 8. For now, you need to look at the speech as a whole piece and read it to yourself without stopping. If it helps, read it to someone you trust. Have that person take notes for you, so you can go back and rewrite anything that needs work.

After you read through it aloud a few times, break the talk into sections and start internalizing the message. The goal is not to memorize the speech. I repeat: don't try to memorize it word for word. The goal of practice is to be comfortable with the material, how it flows, and where you're taking the audience. When it comes to memorization, focus on the key points, ideas, and phrases. The goal is confidence, not perfection. The point of practice is to know where you're going next without having to think about it.

Once you've broken the speech into sections, go paragraph by paragraph to internalize the message. At this point, you need a clear idea of what's coming next and why. Don't move on to the next paragraph until you feel completely comfortable with the one before it. Read paragraph one over and over until you've got it, then move to paragraph two. When you're comfortable with that, go back and do one and two together, and so on. You can do it by paragraph, page, section, whatever differentiation makes sense for your talk. Try to get the spirit of the talk and really know the direction of where it's going. This can seem a little tedious, but such work pays huge dividends when it comes time to perform for an audience.

All of this should be done out loud. Don't look at the page and murmur the lines to yourself; say them as you would in front of a group of people. The point is to hear exactly what it will sound like to an audience. Sometimes it sounds better in your head, so it's important to actually say it aloud. Another way to do this is to record yourself and then listen to the speech to better learn the material. Sometimes I record myself reading the speech exactly as it's written and then listen to it a few times to make notes.

After that, practice going through the entire talk exactly as you will perform it. I recommend going through it at least three to five times. Think through your hand gestures, voice inflections, stage movement, and so on. If you're going to be using a handheld mic, it's worth practicing with something to mimic that feel so you can get used to it. Grab a pen or shampoo bottle and put on a show in your living room. When you're going through it and make a mistake, keep going. This will definitely happen live at some point. You will tell a story wrong or say something out of order—it happens to everyone—and you must be able to push through and save the talk. Most likely, no one but you will even notice those slipups anyway. You'll do it much better if you've practiced moving forward with mistakes.

As you do this, time yourself. This is something a lot of speakers forget to do, and it can be a problem if you're booked for a forty-five-minute talk and only have twenty-five minutes' worth of material, especially if you realize this while onstage. The opposite is true, as well, which can be incredibly frustrating for event planners who hate it when speakers go over time. These kinds of oversights push everything back in the schedule and will likely result in your not getting invited back to the event. There are always going to be nuances that may throw off your time slightly in practice versus the real thing, so practice staying on time as much as possible. Often, speeches start a few minutes late, the person introducing you may take a minute or two longer than expected, you may even have to wait for the okay from the client to go on, and so on. Sometimes there's a ten-minute Q&A with the previous speaker that cuts into your speech time. Consider all these things when you're writing your presentation and timing yourself. You can't anticipate everything, but you can practice keeping your talk tight and even experiment with it going shorter than expected. In my experience, it's easier for a speaker to go over time than to end the speech early. So if you have thirty minutes of material but suddenly need to take up forty minutes, you can usually slow down and spread it out. It's much more difficult to fit forty minutes of material into a thirty-minute slot. So when in doubt, err on the side of brevity.

My friend Chris Ducker is a highly sought-after public speaker who has given hundreds of speeches over the years and now hosts his own events. I once asked Chris about his speech preparation process, and he said that he practices a speech at least twenty-five to thirty times "in performance mode" before he ever once does it live. Such a process helps him refine his material faster, because he knows his delivery is always on point, so if a joke or story falls flat, he scratches it. I can't overemphasize the importance of practicing your talk as much as humanly possible, and Chris's example gives you an idea of how dedicated a professional speaker is to his craft.

Forty-eight hours before your talk, you should be practicing your speech as much as possible. Obviously, you should practice further out than that, but if you do most of your practicing too far in advance, a lot of what you've learned will fade away. I go over the entire talk once more as close as possible to when I speak, without feeling rushed. Sometimes this means doing it in my hotel room before I go backstage or even while I pace backstage. I always want it to be as fresh in my mind as possible.

Frequently Asked Questions about Practice

Over the years, I've received countless questions on speaking, performance, and practice. Here are some of the most popular questions and my answers to them:

1. *Should I video myself?* Videoing yourself can definitely help you identify certain tics or "safety phrases" you often repeat without realizing it. A safety phrase is any phrase you fall back on and use as a filler or crutch, like "um" or "you know" or "Does that make sense?" If you start listening

closely to the people you know, you'll realize we all have them. Maybe you have a weird hand motion you don't like or look down too much. All of this is good to know, and reviewing a video of yourself speaking can help you recognize these things. That said, if videoing yourself isn't an option, don't let that hold you back. It can be helpful but not necessary to the preparation process.

2. *Should I practice in front of other people?* This is different for everybody but is usually not necessary. I typically don't do this, but a lot of people do. If you're going to practice in front of other people, just make sure it's people you really know and trust whose feedback you value. Practicing in front of the wrong people who may encourage or discourage you in the wrong things is more harmful than just doing it by yourself.

3. *Should I practice in front of a mirror?* Michael Port, whom I mentioned earlier, is a professionally trained actor and trains people specifically on the performance side of speaking, and he discourages people from doing this. Typically, I don't do this. Sometimes if I'm telling a story or joke that requires a certain facial expression, like a big cheesy smile, I will look in the mirror and see if it's coming off the way I want it to. Using a mirror in cases like this can be a good idea, but don't get too hung up on it, as you can focus too much on your gestures, facial expressions, etc., and become too self-conscious when speaking. The message is the main thing, not the way you look delivering it.

Notes or No Notes?

The more notes you use, the less genuine your presentation will feel. Most professional speakers do not use notes. I know this may seem intimidating at first, especially if you're just getting started, but if you can't internalize the message of your talk, why should your audience? If you're just reading something to them, it sends the message that you're not that into it, don't care, or simply haven't prepared enough.

One way to get away from using too many notes is to boil your talk down to a handful of key words. The audience doesn't have a script. They won't know if you mess up (unless you tell them, which you won't because now you've practiced moving forward when you mess up). Although most professionals don't use extensive notes, many speakers will use a few notecards with just a handful of key words on them to glance at throughout the presentation in case they lose track of where they are in the talk. Here is an example of one of my forty-five-minute talks, boiled down to key words that help remind me of what I want to say and a few phrases I want to remember to communicate:

Work determines worth	*Day off*
Competitive	*Work finished*
Busyness	*Nothing*
Capacity	*Can't*
Boundaries vs margin	*Fully present*
Outlet	*Who greater than what*
Fun	

All of that probably looks like nonsense to you, but I can do an entire keynote based on that list of words. They each remind me of a point or a story, and I can do the whole presentation with just these words as cues. This is a great strategy if you need something to help keep you focused, or if it just makes you feel better to have it with you. When you're up there onstage, you may find you don't even need the list, but it's a nice security blanket to give you the confidence you need to do the talk well.

Right before You Step Onstage

Before you step onstage, having what I call a "pregame routine" can really help calm your nerves, reduce stress, and prepare you for what's to come. Here's how it works.

Give yourself plenty of travel time. Avoid flying in the day of the presentation, as delays can set you back considerably and you never know what could happen if you're getting in just before your speech. You want to give yourself time to get there on time and have some margin in case something unexpected happens. Of course, this may depend on what time you are speaking and how far you are traveling, but if you're flying in the day of the event and there are any weather issues, missed connections, etc., you're going to be in trouble. Travel stress leads to speaking stress. If you're cutting it short and dealing with issues, that is going to translate into your talk. Always try to think far enough ahead that you're not cutting it too close. The worst thing that can happen is you miss the event.

As soon as you arrive in the town where you're speaking, let the client know. Maybe you've booked this event weeks

WHAT TO DO BEFORE YOU STEP ONSTAGE

or months in advance and haven't had any interaction with the client for some time, and they are trusting that you'll show up (which shouldn't happen, by the way, if you follow the pre-event call protocol outlined in chapter 16). A quick text or email from you will help reduce stress and be one less thing the client has to worry about. When I do this, I usually just say, "Hey, looking forward to seeing you tomorrow. Just wanted to let you know that I'm here." I've had many clients over the years tell me that this simple, thoughtful action made a huge difference.

Once onsite, go see the client. When I arrive at an event, I immediately want to check in with the client and visit the room where I'll be speaking to get a sense of the stage and room setup. If there are any potential issues, I want to know before I start speaking. Not too long ago I was doing a workshop at a conference. We were supposed to have about 100 or 150 people there, but when I got to the room, there were no chairs. That's the kind of thing I like to get figured out ahead of time instead of being ambushed with it right before I speak. I bet you'll want to do the same. That's why having a pregame routine is important.

The final part of a pregame routine is to go through your pre-event checklist:

- *Don't stay up late the night before.* This seems obvious, but it's very important to get a good night's sleep before you speak. Sleep works wonders and can be the difference between you being kind of slow and groggy during your talk and being "on."
- *Don't eat a heavy meal.* You don't want to feel sluggish when you step onstage, so be careful not to

eat too much food before you speak. I usually eat something light just to give me some energy without weighing me down too much. I have a friend who doesn't eat at all the day he speaks, so everybody's different. But in general, a big meal will slow you down, so try to keep it light.

- *Set out clothes ahead of time.* One time I didn't do this, and as I was getting ready to speak, I realized my shirt was missing a button. At that point, there was nothing to do but go onstage and hope nobody noticed. Another time I pulled out my shoes and they were mismatched, two right shoes from two different pairs. My wife happened to be with me that time and went out to buy me a new pair of shoes. The point is, you just want to get this stuff done ahead of time so you're not in a bind.

- *Review your talk one more time.* Practice it the way you will perform it but at about 50 percent of the energy one last time to boost your confidence and get as comfortable as possible. Why 50 percent? Because you want to save everything you have for onstage where you can go all out; plus, you don't want to exhaust yourself right before the gig. Since you've seen the room now, think through the stage and setup. Think through your pauses, movements, and gestures. You're just working on your muscle memory so that when you get up on the stage it's natural. If you're driving, just talk to yourself out loud on the way.

- *Run a tech rehearsal.* Some of the bigger venues may actually schedule you for a sound check or tech run-through, but regardless, you need to check your sound before you get onstage. Most venues and event planners don't give a lot of thought to this. They usually just tell you it's going to be fine. I've had plenty of times when they tell me it will be no big deal and I end up with mic issues. You always want to check it yourself if you can.

- *See how the stage is lit.* When you're doing a mic check, all the house lights will probably be up. But if there will be some special type of stage lights, ask if the tech people can show you what it will be like. Anything you can do to get a feel for exactly what it will be like is helpful. You don't want to be blinded walking onstage if you aren't expecting it. That comes across as unprofessional. Every speaker has his or her own preference, but I prefer the house lights up a bit so I can see the audience. That's called a "stage wash" as opposed to a spotlight.
- *Review slides if you're using them.* If you're using a slide advancer (aka a "clicker"), practice with it and see how long it takes to actually advance to the next slide so you can time your transitions and speaking.
- *Walk the stage.* Get a feel for its size. Look around and see where everyone will be seated. If there are going to be cameras, make sure you know where they are so you can look at them every once in a while.
- *Arrive at the venue an hour early.* Walk around the room and sit in a couple different areas to get an idea of what the audience will see. It's a very different view if you're sitting in the front row versus the

last row, and you should know what each perspective looks like to the audience. Go over with the client one last time when you are expected to go onstage and how long you have for your talk. You will have gone over this already, but I like to hammer out that stuff one more time just to make sure nothing has changed. Sometimes they have to cut your time down at the last minute. If possible, meet with members of the audience. This is a personal preference for me, but it calms my nerves a bit to talk with attendees of the event. It's always good to remember that the audience members are just people.

- *Drink a little water*—and I mean a *little* water. You don't want to need to use the bathroom while onstage. Hot tea or room temperature water is great for your vocal chords, whereas cold water can sometimes strain them. Honey is great for the throat if you want to make sure it doesn't get too dry. Try to steer clear of caffeinated beverages like coffee that will dehydrate you and make you have to go to the bathroom.

- *Check your teeth and your fly* (and no, I'm not joking about this). Chris Ducker was in Philadelphia giving a popular keynote at a national conference for speakers. Naturally, he nailed the talk, but there was a woman in the front row who kept staring at him through the entire presentation, hardly taking her eyes off him. "I'm not that good-looking," Chris later joked, "so there must have been a problem." After the speech, he was talking with guests and signing books when the woman came up to him and said,

"I really enjoyed your speech, I took lots of mental notes, but I'm not sure if you're aware or not, but your zipper was flying low." He looked down, and lo and behold, there was his zipper still in the down position, and it had been for the entire presentation. Now the last thing he does before stepping onstage is take a quick glance down just to make sure. I suggest you do the same.

If you have prepared well for your speech, you're ready. You've done the work. Now it's time to deliver the goods.

ACTION PLAN

1. Study the talk. Rehearse it out loud to familiarize yourself with the content.

2. Deliver the talk as you would in front of an audience.

3. Time yourself to make sure you do it in the time you're allotted for the gig.

4. Create a pregame ritual and checklist for speaking gigs.

> BONUS: To download a checklist template for speaking gigs, go to SpeakerBookBonus.com.

7

How to Use Technology and Other Tools

Depending on how you use it, technology can be your best friend or your worst enemy when delivering a talk. If you decide to use such tools in your presentation, they should be used as enhancements to the presentation, not as replacements for it. Here's a litmus test to see if you're relying too heavily on tech: If you couldn't use any technology in your talk, would it still be good? If you get to the venue and your slides won't come up or the music won't play, is your talk still worth delivering? If not, then you have a problem. The speech needs to be able to stand on its own without any slides or tools or technological wizardry. That's why I stress starting with building a great talk that you rehearse over and over again. Then you can decide if adding technology makes sense. Don't begin with needing to use a song or video or slide deck. Always start with the talk. It's your greatest asset.

HOW TO USE TECHNOLOGY AND OTHER TOOLS

In this chapter, we're going to look at the most common technology tools speakers use and the pros and cons of them, as well as the best times to use them.

Slides

Slides are any images or text that appear on a screen while you are delivering your talk. The upside of using slides is that your notes are on the screen, so it's easy to know where you're going. They can be a great enhancement for key points as well. Certain points make a bigger impact when you show a picture while making your point. They can also be useful for getting the audience to laugh.

The downside of using slides is that, like any technology, they may not work. The setup may not have what you need in terms of software or connection cables. The room may be too big for people to see the slides, something may be wrong with the screen, or any number of other things could go wrong. Factors like these can cause more stress and throw off the rest of your presentation, so just know that when using slides, you're adding another variable to the equation. If you're going to use slides, use them to reinforce what you're already saying. Never read off of them verbatim, and be sure to stay focused on the audience when showing the slides. You should always know what the next slide is so you don't have to look at the screen. Don't let the use of slides be an excuse for not practicing your talk.

When using slides, here are a few key things to remember:

- *Avoid using stock images, which are often impersonal and boring.* Either use custom images that have been designed by a designer or even use your own images, which may come from your cell phone. The point is to convey the personality of the speaker in the presentation, including the slides.

- *Less is more.* Try to keep any words you use on the slides to short sentences and bullet points. Don't include too much or your audience will focus their attention on your slides instead of on you.
- *Arrive at the venue early to test your slides.* When Bill Gates was rolling out Windows 98, he was presenting the new technology to a large conference and got an error message midpresentation. You don't want this to happen to you, so make sure you test your slides beforehand. Everything in your presentation should be big enough to be seen by anyone in the room, and if there's video, be sure to test the audio beforehand as well. Leave nothing to chance.
- *Get your own remote.* Regard this tool as an extension of your own hand. Don't leave it on a podium or somewhere onstage and run back and forth every time to advance your slides. That's not fun to watch and distracts the audience from the real presentation.

Props, Visuals, and Handouts

As with slides, you may use props and visuals in your presentation as an enhancement of the material in your talk, but not as a replacement. Your speech needs to stand alone without the use of any visuals apart from delivering it. That way if something goes wrong, the show can still go on.

Props work well to emphasize a point, but they're not great on their own. In a talk I do on how busy our lives are, I take a clear glass and start filling it with water while rattling off all the things we usually have going on in our lives. I have the audience chime in with the things they're balancing in life, such as work, friends, relationships, and so on. Often, the people in the audience are shouting them out and I just keep pouring until the glass eventually starts dripping over the sides. Then I talk about what we do when we don't realize we're full and just keep adding more activities and responsibilities. While I'm saying this I continue to pour, which makes a mess and surprises people. They usually laugh nervously, but it makes a great point and sticks in the audience's mind. Obviously, the point works without the use of visuals, but the illustration drives the point home even more.

When using props, remember the following:

- *Make sure everyone in the audience can see the prop.* In one of my talks, I tell a story about an old yearbook of mine, which isn't very big, so I have to plan ahead for that and make sure people can see it when I pull it out. This means asking the event planner how large the audience is and making sure I have a table or another place to set the book so I don't have to hold it the entire time or set it on the floor. Sometimes, with a larger audience, I'll use large, exaggerated gestures and even narrate what I'm doing so people understand what the prop is.
- *Props should create mystery.* You can either leave a prop sitting out on a table that's covered up and then

reveal it or leave it out but don't address it. Mystery is fun and gets the audience thinking, "I wonder what that's about."
- *Practice with your prop.* Script out how you'll introduce it and how to handle it. Will you point to it? Set it somewhere and then go get it? Practice nailing your transition from using the prop to applying it to the message. Think through the nuances of how many hands it will take and if you'll be using a handheld microphone at the time.
- *Consider how to travel with the prop.* If it's big, you may have to get creative. Jeff Jones was the drummer with the band Big Daddy Weave for over thirteen years. Now he is a full-time speaker and entrepreneur who incorporates his drumming experience into his presentations by setting up a kit onstage and doing a solo, which the audience loves. Instead of traveling with a drum set, though, he finds a local church wherever he's traveling and borrows a kit from them. That's a great example of thinking through ahead of time how you'll use your prop.
- *Make it clear why you're using the prop.* You want an obvious application to your speech so people aren't left wondering what that was all about, which ultimately will only distract people.
- *Avoid passing things around the audience.* Not only do you not want your stuff damaged, but it takes people out of the moment. They stop listening to you and instead focus on the prop.

Props can be incredible tools when connected to a powerful point in your presentation. Bill Gates did a TED Talk called "Mosquitoes, Malaria, and Education" in which he has a jar onstage with a few mosquitoes flying around in it. He never references it, building a sense of mystery and intrigue during his speech, until he finally opens the lid and lets a few fly around the room while talking about how dangerous they are. It's both shocking and exciting. Another TED Talk example is when Jamie Oliver mentions how much sugar the average human consumes and then wheels out a wheelbarrow full of sugar cubes, dumping them onstage for everyone to see. And then there's Jill Bolte Taylor's "My Stroke of Insight" TED Talk about having a stroke in which she brings out a human brain and explains the different parts of it. Using a diagram is great, but bringing out an actual brain is even better. That's the power of a prop.

Microphones, Cameras, and Music

There are, of course, other less obvious technology tools. Comedians know this better than most, that the number one prop you have in any presentation is that thing in your hands (or wrapped around your ear). You must make friends with the microphone. What do you do, though, when you're speaking and it decides to hate you? Maybe you're getting ear-piercing feedback or it just flat-out dies. First of all: Don't panic. If it doesn't bother you, it won't bother the audience. If you make a big deal out of it, it will become a big deal to them. Always have a backup plan. Before you step onstage, you may want to ask the tech people if they have a backup mic in case of such an emergency. Regardless, the show must always go on, one way or another, and you should be ready for anything. There are times when the mic just isn't going to work and you will have to improvise by projecting your voice to the audience. This will happen at some point, so practice for it.

Another tool is the use of cameras and screens. In larger venues, there may be a camera crew, in which case the majority of the audience may be watching you on a screen. If this is the case, you should talk directly to the camera for parts of your presentation so the audience feels you are looking at them. Sometimes the crew moves around, so try to have a sense of that. Let the crew know ahead of time if they need to zoom in at any specific times in your speech. If they need a close-up picture or you're going to call someone up from the audience, they should know that ahead of time.

Music is also a great tool for creating energy, especially before a session starts. Often the event will be playing music before you go on or while you're being introduced. They may even ask if you have a preference, so always have a "walk-on song" ready. Music works well in workshops too. If people are in small discussion groups, having some instrumental music playing in the background can help with concentration. It's a great tool to set the mood, get the creativity flowing, and help people focus on the discussion.

The Forgotten Tool: The Room

The environment is one of the biggest factors in how well a presentation goes and one of the most overlooked "tools" in a presentation. But the truth is that the room is, in fact, a form of technology you need to know how to use. If the environment is set up poorly, this can have a huge impact on you and the crowd. If it is set up right, that can make a world of difference for your presentation, turning a lukewarm audience into an awesome crowd. It's your job as the speaker to do everything you can to stack the deck in your favor. Often the event planner hasn't chosen a venue based on how optimal it is for speaking. Sometimes it's just what they could afford or all that was available, so it's your responsibility to make sure the room works for your presentation and vice versa.

When considering the room, you'll want to concentrate on three main areas: size, seating, and lighting.

Room Size

Ideally, the room should feel almost too small for the audience. A packed room creates a lot of energy and excitement for the event. That's the law of the crowd: If you walk into an event that seems crowded, people feed off that energy and it feels like the place to be. Once I was at a conference where the room was set up for 1,200 people and there were close to 1,300 there. The client was nervous, but I told him not to worry because that was perfect. The bigger and emptier a room, the more it will swallow up the audience and energy. Having a packed room is not a problem at all; it's the perfect recipe for an engaged group of people who are ready to receive whatever you share with them.

Years ago, I did a keynote at a conference for around 3,000 people. We were in a huge industrial building, and it worked fine for a keynote, but right after that, they wanted me to do a workshop in that same room for 100 people.

Those are two very different dynamics. It was way too big a room for only 100 people, but ultimately we had to find a way to make it work. If you have any say over where you deliver your talk, make sure that you are always presenting to a full room. If necessary, take away chairs, rope off sections of the venue, or do whatever needs to be done. The feeling of a full room is the difference between an engaged audience and a dead one.

Seating Setup

Another factor to consider when paying attention to the room is seating setup. In general, you will want people as close to you and to each other as possible. Crowd density is your best friend, as energy, laughter, and engagement are all contagious. When people are in close quarters, they start to mimic each other, so if I can make one person laugh, I can get the rest of the crowd to join in. That's why laugh tracks exist; they trigger others to laugh as well. Sometimes you don't have any control over this; sometimes you do. In the example of doing a workshop right after speaking to 3,000 people in an auditorium, it was unrealistic to tear down 2,900 chairs in ten minutes, so we simply had everyone move down to the first few rows. Often you can make suggestions like this to the event planner, which ultimately helps everyone involved, including yourself.

If you get to the venue and see way more seats than audience members, don't freak out. This, incidentally, is why you always want to arrive early. At this point, your goal is to get everybody to move to the front and center, however that can most easily and practically be done. Sometimes, you can ask the host or emcee to ask everyone to move; other times, you have to do it yourself. Some people won't like this, and they may even grumble a bit, but do it anyway, knowing that it's for their own good. You can ask someone to stand at the door and give instructions to people as they walk in, or you can rope off certain rows. Whatever you do, the point is to shrink the room to increase engagement and energy, which will result in a better presentation for everyone.

If you're giving a keynote and the event planner asks about tables, let them know your preference is to not have tables in the audience. There are some situations where there's a good reason to use them, but in general they create dead space and take away from crowd density. In some workshop settings where people need computers or are taking lots of notes, it's appropriate to have tables in the audience. In these situations you should ask for rectangular tables to be set up so that everyone is facing the same direction. With circular tables, half the people would have their backs to you during your presentation, and they would have to turn around to see you, which would just be uncomfortable.

Remember: you want everyone as close to the stage as possible. Also, the purpose of the stage is so everyone can see you, but if it's not necessary, don't use it. Do not feel confined to the stage; feel free to move to a place where the audience gets the best experience. Find ways to close the gap between you and the audience, which may mean moving offstage at some point. If you plan to do this, consider any potential audio, visual, or tech issues that may arise (camera shot, lighting, microphone cable, audio feedback, etc.). Test all this in your sound check before doing your live presentation so there are no surprises.

Lighting

Every speaker has a preference for lighting. In general, I recommend that your lighting be as bright as possible without washing you out. The point of lighting is for people to see you. When you're walking the stage, make sure you know where you can stand while still being fully in the light. The more people have to strain to see you, the more they get drowsy and tune you out. Instead of a spotlight, I recommend a "stage wash," which I mentioned earlier means having the house lights up a bit. This will allow you to see the audience's faces and create a stronger connection with them.

When it comes to getting your ideal room setup, be sure to ask for what you need ahead of time. In my speaking contract (which we will discuss in chap. 15), I use a basic rider to give them a heads-up of my different technology preferences including what type of microphone I like, the best type of lighting for me, and so on. The goal here is to not be demanding but to make the presentation the best it can be. You're setting yourself up for success without being a diva.

Some of my best presentations have happened not because I did anything different in my speech—I told all the same stories and points—but because the environment was rigged for me to succeed. Don't overlook the importance of this tool in your kit of resources that will help you succeed as a speaker.

What to Wear

There are no hard-and-fast rules regarding attire for events. Every speaker and event is different. Some events, like awards banquets, may require formal attire (or what I call "fancy clothes"), whereas others will welcome a far more casual approach to how you dress. Aside from client expectations, this is mostly a matter of personal preference. Some speakers like dressing up for every event they go to no matter what, and others prefer to dress down. That said, here are some practical ways to think through what you wear to a speaking gig.

The easiest approach is to simply match the audience. This is a pretty safe bet, but it may require you to bring a few options since you won't know what the audience is wearing until you get there. Another idea is to dress a step above the audience. If they are in business casual, you may want to be a little dressier, since the goal is to look professional. The audience is making assumptions about you even before you speak, so you want to be intentional with what you wear, as it will communicate a certain impression.

Some speakers do their own thing and wear what fits their style. This only works with more well-known speakers who can get away with doing what they want. For example, I know a speaker who always wears a black T-shirt and jeans, regardless of the setting. But he can do that because he's in demand and people know what they're getting. I know another guy who always wears western-style button-up shirts because that's what he likes. The comedian Gabriel Iglesias only wears shorts and a Hawaiian shirt because that's part of his brand. But for regular people like you and me, and for those who are just getting started, it's a risk to do this before you have an established brand. If you show up in shorts and flip-flops, chances are you won't get booked again.

When in doubt, ask the event planner what attire the audience will be in and what the expectations of the event are. I ask this at two different times: first in the pre-event form I send and then in the pre-event call we do a week or two before the event. My preference is to be comfortable but classy, which usually means nice jeans and a button-up shirt, but if the client insists I wear a suit, I do that. Keeping the client happy is our first job. When in doubt, err on the side of caution and being conservative. Similar to using humor, you don't want to do anything that may be considered inappropriate or offensive to the person signing your check.

Also, be careful of crazy patterns. At larger events, you may appear on video, so you should wear solid colors and avoid lots of stripes and checkered patterns. When you dress in non-solids, it can be more difficult for the video camera to register you, and you may even look funky when you move around.

When rehearsing your talk, do at least one run-through in your stage outfit so you get a feel for your movements and gestures. This is especially important for women who may be wearing a dress or heels, but even if you're wearing a suit and dress shoes, your movements will be significantly different than if you are in casual clothes. You don't want to be limited in your mobility or realize you've got a wardrobe malfunction when you raise your arms. Practice everything. If you sweat a lot onstage, you'll want to know this ahead of time and consider an appropriate shirt color. While practicing, be mindful of choices in accessories such as jewelry, which can be noisy and move around quite a bit. When in doubt, keep it simple. Your wardrobe is yet another tool that should complement your talk, not distract from it.

Finally, remember to do a last-minute check before you go onstage. Check your teeth, your fly, and your backside to make sure everything looks good. I once watched a speaker give a whole presentation with his suit jacket tucked into the back of his pants. If I couldn't stop looking at it, I know everyone else felt the same way.

Lecterns and Podiums

As a general rule, it's a bad idea to stand behind a podium, which creates a divide between you and the audience. That said, there are some scenarios when it may be appropriate to use a podium.

One such time would be when you need to read an in-depth quote or a statistic and want to make sure it is accurate. If you're using a physical prop, it may also make sense to set the item on the podium and come back to it when needed. If the event space already has a podium or lectern, make sure it's not in the middle of the stage, and if it is, move it. If it can't be moved, just work around it, which is a reality of some venues. I've had to do this plenty of times, especially in churches, where the lectern is often a permanent fixture of the stage. If it's not too close to the edge of the stage, just walk in front of it. You can also use the podium as a prop, leaning on it or even setting something on it. Just don't stand behind it with your hands gripping it.

People who use podiums or lecterns are often reading their notes, and it makes them feel comfortable to hide behind something. It's a safety net. If you need a podium, what you really need is more practice.

ACTION PLAN

1. Decide if you will use slides for your presentation. If so, create them using the rules mentioned in this chapter.

2. Choose appropriate visuals and props that help illustrate part of your talk.

3. Get to the venue early enough to check out the environment and do what you can to make the room ideal for your presentation. Density is your friend.

4. Decide what to wear. When in doubt, just be professional.

> BONUS: For more help with the use of technology and other tools in your presentation, visit SpeakerBookBonus.com.

8

How to Deliver a Talk without Boring Your Audience to Tears

In 2000 the average attention span of a human was twelve seconds. In 2013 it dropped to eight seconds, one second shorter than that of a goldfish. These days it's practically impossible for people to be fully present for long periods of time due to the many devices and media pulling our attention in different directions. Our minds are often stuck in the past or concerned with the future, sometimes both at the same time. We may catch ourselves thinking, "As soon as I'm done here I've got to run this errand and then I need to talk to that person and check my email." There's always something else to do.

As a speaker, it's getting harder and harder to hold people's interest while you speak. You rarely have their complete attention, which is why it's even more important to deliver an engaging presentation. In this chapter, we'll explore how to do just that, using speaking dynamics and audience participation to keep people engaged through your entire talk. Though distractions abound, it's possible to speak to an audience who pays attention to your every word.

So where do we start?

What You Can Do to Engage People

Before we talk about the audience, let's talk about you and how you can make your speech as dynamic as possible. In addition to using props and visuals, as we previously discussed, you can also focus on a few important dynamics that can significantly affect how your audience receives the message.

First, start the talk with a strong opening. If you don't capture the attention of your audience in the first five minutes, you will likely lose them forever. Those few moments are when they are most engaged and you have the greatest opportunity to earn their trust. Don't squander it. When you start speaking, people are listening intently because they don't know where this is headed. It's a lot like the start of a roller coaster: There's that anticipation during those first few moments as you climb the hill with each clack-clack of the tracks. What will happen next? What twists and turns will we take? Where will this lead? The not knowing is exciting; it could be awesome or boring, and those first few minutes of your talk will clue them in to how the rest will go.

In the first five minutes, you have to hook the audience because their attention spans will only go downhill from there. This is why TED Talks range in length from eight to twenty minutes and why they almost always begin with a strong story or some surprising statement. They know people have limited brain space, and those first few seconds of a talk shouldn't be wasted on introductions or some anecdote about how you got there. The most exciting part of a talk is at the very beginning, and how you spend this time will, in many ways, determine how successful you are.

Second, make your energy match the room. The bigger the room, the bigger you need to make everything you do: gestures, movements, pauses, emphasis on key points, volume, etc. Don't shrink onstage. How you present to an audience of ten should be different from how you present to an audience of a hundred. And the same applies with going from a hundred to a thousand. When talking to a smaller crowd, they can see and hear everything you do pretty easily, but when speaking to a larger crowd, everyone has a harder time seeing and sometimes hearing, so you need to step it up. This can be uncomfortable, so don't try to be something you're not. Just be a passionate, fully present version of yourself. As the size of your audience grows, your whole presentation needs to grow and the intensity should increase, without sacrificing your style or personality.

Third, make use of opening and closing loops. Opening a loop means you're raising a question in the audience's mind that makes them want to keep listening. For example, if I say, "In just a couple minutes I'm going to share with you the biggest mistake new speakers make onstage that you can avoid," I've just opened a loop. The audience will want to keep listening because they want to know the answer. TV shows do this a lot, leaving you with a cliff-hanger at the end of an episode to keep you coming back. Opening and closing loops throughout your presentation is a great way to keep the audience engaged, sometimes without them even realizing it. Just make sure you close all the loops you open, or it will confuse people.

In addition to doing what you can do to create an engaging presentation, you can ask the audience to do things as well.

Getting the Audience Involved

A good presentation is a dialogue between the speaker and the audience. The audience might not be speaking back to you, but they're involved. You may be the one with the microphone, but seeking ways to get your audience involved will keep them engaged the whole time. There are a variety of techniques you can use, but below are six of the best ways to get an audience involved. I've shared them here in order of increasing levels of trust required, with the first being the easiest and the last being the hardest:

1. *Ask for a show of hands.* Use this right out of the gate, because it's a low-pressure way to get people involved and a good way to check the pulse of an audience. You can ask how many people are there for the first time, who traveled more than three hours to get there, who had coffee this morning, etc. You might even tweak some of your material based on their answers. It's also helpful to throw out a "softball question" that everyone will raise their hand for, like "How many people have had a job that they hated?" The goal is to get as many people as possible involved, so asking multiple questions helps.

2. *Call and response.* This is similar to hand raising except you're asking the audience to audibly answer. You might say, "How many of you have ever had a bad day? Let me hear you say 'that's me.'" In the past when speaking to student audiences, I would say, "If you can hear me, clap twice." If you use this technique early on in your talk and keep coming back to it, people will catch on. My friend Mike does a great job letting the audience finish his sentences by leaving out the last word and allowing the audience to fill it in. That's call and response.
3. *Get people to answer your question.* Do this several minutes into your talk after you've built some trust, giving them parameters to make it easier to answer and to discourage long-winded answers that can sometimes derail your talk. Whenever I speak at colleges, I ask students to give me a one-word adjective to describe the stereotypical college student. When people answer, always repeat what they said, because some won't have heard it. If you ask a question and no one responds, acknowledge the silence. Sometimes you can make it funny, but the longer you stand there waiting, the more awkward it will become. If still no one responds, move on.
4. *Get people moving.* Have them stand up, stretch, do jumping jacks, or move around the room. This gets people's blood pumping and acts as a little break that helps them refocus. You could also ask them to high five each other or say something to their neighbor—anything fun that creates a sense of camaraderie.

Obviously use your discretion here as this may be appropriate in certain settings and not in others. If you're interested in doing a movement exercise, be sure to ask the client ahead of time if this would be appropriate and let them know what you're planning.

5. *Encourage group discussion.* If you know of an interesting challenge or problem that relates to your topic, this is a great way to pose it to your audience and find out what they think. Just know how much discussion time you want to give them and the complexity of the problem. You don't want to use this as a replacement for the bulk of your talk, nor do you want to ask them to end world hunger in five minutes. Keep the group size small, around five people, which allows everyone to have a chance to talk. This can work for lots of settings but is most common in workshops and seminars.

6. *Invite people to role-play onstage.* This is the highest form of audience participation and the most difficult to pull off. You can bring a volunteer onstage to act something out. This can work really well or be a huge disaster. Try to set it up for success by prepping a volunteer beforehand and pick a person who will play along but not steal the show. When you bring someone onstage, you are sharing some of your power with him or her, so be careful with that and be willing to improvise if it doesn't go exactly as planned.

The more you speak, the better you'll become at reading the room and the audience to know which interactions will work in which settings. Part of your job is not just to do what you wanted to do going into the gig, but to feel out the audience and decide what's best for them.

Audience Q&A

Q&A usually happens at the end of a presentation and tends to leave an impression, so it's something you should prepare for. But when should you do it? First, it depends on the type of talk you do. Q&A is more common in a workshop setting, but you can do it for keynotes and seminars as well, depending on the goal of the talk. Personally, I always do Q&A in workshops and almost never in keynotes. It may also depend on the size of the audience. In general, the bigger the audience, the harder it is to do Q&A. It depends on the length of your talk too. If you don't have much time, you may not get to do it at all. And lastly, it depends on how engaged the audience is. Sometimes people don't have any questions, and usually this is something you can tell before you get to the end of your presentation.

Doing audience Q&A is both fun and a little scary. Anything can happen, but that doesn't mean it has to be intimidating. It's a great way to answer questions from people in your audience and learn what they want to hear about. If you regularly hear the same questions, that's valuable information because you can modify your presentation to include that information.

I frequently do a webinar on teaching and speaking, and when I first started doing that presentation, I kept hearing the same questions over and over during the Q&A. For example, I got specific questions about demo videos, so I modified that section of the training to address those. People also regularly wanted to know about speaking fees, so I added a section about that.

If you decide to have a Q&A, here are some guidelines:

- Ask people to raise their hand. Don't let them just shout out questions, which can get chaotic. Also, just because someone has their hand up doesn't mean you have to call on them. Sometimes you may just get a vibe from someone that they could be hostile or rude. You have the right to not call on that person.
- Always repeat the question for the audience, because there will always be someone who didn't hear the question.
- Keep your answers short and sweet so you can get to more questions.
- Expect the unexpected. Because you can't completely prepare for this, surprises will happen. The more you do this, though, the better you'll get at handling these situations. You may have someone who wants to take over the mic or ask too many questions. You may have someone who is too aggressive or trying to be controversial or just plain rude. This person is probably annoying the audience and not just you, so tell them to see you afterward to continue the conversation. It's a good way to get them to sit down without explicitly telling them to be quiet. You can also use this technique if someone asks a question that isn't relevant to what you've said.

- Know how to handle a rambling question. Usually, people asking a question like this are just nervous and having trouble formulating complete sentences. Don't be afraid to interrupt them. You're not being rude if you do this; you're helping them get to the point, and you're saving them from themselves. One way to do this is to ask, "What's your question?" as kindly as you can and with a smile. It took courage for them to ask a question, so don't embarrass them. But they may need some redirection. You could also ask, "How can I best help you today?" If the person has already asked a question but is going on and on with unnecessary context, just jump in and say, "All right, so if I'm hearing you correctly, your question is . . ." Summarize it, answer, and move on.
- Offer your contact information to allow people to follow up with you. Use your discretion here and don't give out any sensitive information, but this is a great way to stay in touch with an audience and respond to any questions you didn't have time to answer. Also, if you're just trying to get someone to give up the mic, telling them to contact you at your business address is a great way to move them on without being rude.
- Be ready to interrupt and redirect. Sometimes people want to get up and share their own advice. This is fine as long as it is concise and to the point. If they keep going on, though, you may have to interrupt with a question or redirect their statement. If they're going on about something completely irrelevant, you

can suggest, "Interesting thoughts there. I appreciate that. Let's stay on the current topic for right now." Never make fun of them; just redirect.

- Don't be afraid to say, "I don't know." What do you do if you are asked an impossible question? Maybe it's too profound or you just don't know. Never be afraid to say, "That's a great question. I'm not really sure." You don't know everything, so don't act like you do. You could also pose it to the audience and ask if they have any thoughts. If you're in a room with other speakers you know, you could throw it to them as well and ask if they have a good answer.

- No matter what, be kind. You may get cornered after a presentation by someone who won't stop talking or asking you questions. When this happens, as annoying as it may sometimes be, say to the person, "Help me understand your question here," or "How can I best help you?" You can always give him or her your email or a way to follow up that's simpler, but be sensitive to the person. It's a privilege that people want to talk to you; never forget that. You could say, "It sounds like we have a lot to talk about, would you catch me in a little bit after I talk to these other people? I want to make sure I have the chance to chat with them." Never be afraid to excuse yourself for another commitment. If you have to be somewhere else, you can always let people walk with you and then say goodbye when it's time to go.

Three Factors That Affect Attention

Which technique should you use and when? You can be the best speaker in the world and still lose people's attention. You're up against human nature, which almost always wins, so switching things up and creating audience involvement helps keep their attention and allows them to retain more of the talk. The kinds of audience involvement are largely based on three factors.

- *The size of the audience.* The bigger the crowd, the harder it is to interact with people. You can always ask people to raise their hands, which works in any setting. You can also have people turn and have a conversation with their neighbor or break people up into small groups to discuss something. This all becomes increasingly challenging with a larger audience, so keep that in mind as you consider which techniques to use for your audience.
- *The type of presentation.* As a general rule, the longer you speak, the more interactions you should have with your audience. If I'm doing a forty-five-minute keynote, I may just have a few interactions here and there. But if I'm doing a three-hour workshop, I'm going to need a lot more interaction.
- *The size of the room.* We touched on this in the last chapter, but not only does the size of the room affect the feel of your talk, it can also limit or allow audience members to move around. If the room configuration allows, sometimes I have the audience get up and spread out for an activity or to form groups.

If they're in a room that's absolutely packed, that makes it difficult. Again, just be aware of the room when you're deciding what kinds of activities you want the audience to participate in.

Your audience involvement is a direct result of how much trust you've earned. At the beginning of a talk you have no rapport, you haven't built trust yet. It's hard to get the audience to do anything more than simply raise their hands. People's internal dialogue is, "We just met and you're already asking me to do stuff? You're the speaker, you're the one who's supposed to be doing stuff." That's why you always want to start with a strong opening that doesn't rely on the audience. As you build rapport through smaller interactions, though, it becomes easier to get them involved.

What to Do When Things Go Wrong

Public speaking is a performance and things can and will go wrong no matter how good you are. No matter how much you practice, there are always factors outside of your control that can affect how people respond (or don't). Here are some of the things that can go wrong and how to handle them.

- *Nobody is listening.* Most audiences are at least respectful enough to pretend they are listening, but there will always be some who are checked out. As a rule, focus on the people who are fully engaged, not those who aren't listening to you. Pay attention to the people who are nodding, leaning forward, and taking notes. Those are the ones who want to be there and whom you are most likely to impact. But as an audience naturally drifts, one way to reel them back in is to say, "Hey everybody, look up here for a second." I'll say that for key points, not to scold anyone or point out they're not paying attention. It can disarm an audience and clue them back in to what you're doing. When you do this, try putting down the microphone for a minute and just shout, which can be effective in small doses. You can also do this for really passionate points, but only for a short period of time. Put down the mic and say your point really loudly to change the volume and feel of the room. Not only does it shake things up, but without the mic between you and the audience, it can help people feel more connected.

- *Your allotted time gets cut.* I spoke at a conference recently where they hired me to do a morning and afternoon session. The conference was running so far behind all day that I didn't get to present my afternoon session. Those things happen. Conferences are notorious for running off schedule, so try to be preemptive and come up with alternatives, like having shortened versions of your talks prepared ahead of time. Keep confirming with the event planner how much time you have, if anything is getting cut, and when you need to end your talk. Don't be demanding; just be flexible and considerate. Your role is to serve.

- *You get sick.* If at all possible, the show must go on. Everybody is different, and you should follow your doctor's orders, but if you just have a light fever or headache, try to press through. It sounds callous, but part of being a professional is delivering a talk even when it's difficult. That said, when you're not well, try to rest as much as possible and drink plenty of fluids. If you're deathbed ill, keep the client informed and communicate with as much advance notice as possible so they can make arrangements to replace you if necessary.

- *Your time is almost up, but you still have more to say.* The best way to prevent this, of course, is to practice ahead of time. But sometimes you go on late or your pace just ends up being different when you're onstage. Be aware of the clock or timer in the room if there is one. Figure this out ahead of time in sound check or the day before. Sometimes you have an exact amount of time to speak, and sometimes the client doesn't care. Always be ready to abandon the good material for the sake of the great, making sure you hit your main points, even if you have to cut great supporting ideas or stories. If you've come to the end of your time and you're not "done," give people a method to follow up with you, saying something like, "Hey, I had a couple other thoughts I wanted to share so feel free to email me if you want to know more or if you have a question." You can offer to email your slides to everyone so they can see what you didn't get to. Just give them a way to connect afterward.
- *Sometimes clients are jerks.* Ideally you'll recognize this before an event and judge whether it's worth

doing or not. Remember, your job is to serve the client, so tread lightly here. Often the client is not trying to be a jerk; he or she is just stressed or tired. But if the person truly is terrible to work with, do your job, finish strong, and don't work with that client again. Especially at the beginning of your career, referrals and testimonials are important, so don't give the client a reason to say anything bad about you. You don't have to be a pushover, but try to keep the client happy, and then move on.

- *Only five people show up.* I've had this happen before where only one or two people showed up to my session. I won't lie: this can be a big blow to your ego, but it's also a good learning experience. Remember that the audience size determines the dynamic of the presentation, so you will have to adjust. In this case, you will want to switch to a more informal mode of presentation. Maybe drop your slides or put down the mic. Pull the chairs in or circle up to make it more of a discussion than a presentation. Despite being disappointed, relax a bit and be more personal. And no matter what, do the best job you can do.

- *There's a distraction in the room.* This goes back to managing your environment. If you make it a big deal, it will be a big deal. If you ignore it and act like it's not a big deal, the audience will react the same way. But if it becomes unbearable and is affecting people's experience, you have to address it. Once I was speaking and the electricity went out in the building. You can't just ignore that one. Another time I was speaking in a metal building during a hailstorm, and it was so loud, we had to acknowledge it. There may be times when you're speaking in a conference center with portable walls and you can hear everything in the next room. You don't have to pretend it's not happening. It can help relax everyone if you call it out and turn it into a joke. Humor always defuses a tense situation. If the distraction is unavoidable, say something funny about it and move on.

Mitch Joel was speaking at a lunch event in Chicago, and during his speech, everyone was eating and talking, not paying attention. Mitch was using every tool in his toolbox to keep people engaged, but none of it was working. "When I do speeches," he said, "I'm talking, but I'm also thinking about what to do with my hands, where to walk, etc. I'm thinking as I speak. But in this case I had another voice in my head saying, 'Man, it's loud in here! I can't believe how loud it is!'" The event organizer even came onstage at one point and pleaded with the crowd to pay attention.

Despite all the noise and distractions, Mitch just kept doing his thing and plowed on like a professional. Nothing went as planned, and nobody listened. Even someone as successful and in-demand as Mitch has bad events. Later when he was putting together an updated speaker reel for his website, most of it was from that event. He was giving so much effort to try to get people's attention, it turned out that it was the best video of him speaking. The lesson here is, don't panic when things go wrong and don't let a little opposition get you down. You never know what may happen.

Dealing with Tough Audiences

Tough audiences do not mean you are a bad speaker—it's just part of the job. There's a big difference in the dynamic between audiences who want to be there and those who have to be there. If possible, it's best to know this ahead of time and prepare accordingly, but sometimes you just have to deal with it.

Early on in my career as a youth speaker, I spoke at a lot of school assemblies, which is the kind of audience who has to be there. One gig was at a high school assembly on a Friday afternoon before spring break. The only thing standing between them and their freedom was me. Can you imagine the glares I got? To top it off, right in the middle of the presentation there was an announcement on the loudspeaker telling the volleyball team it was time to get ready for their game. At that point, thirty girls stood up all at once and walked. It wasn't my best presentation, but I had to keep going. Those kinds of things are out of your control, and one of the greatest skills a speaker has is the ability to keep going.

Sometimes I've spoken at mandatory training seminars that the audiences may not be thrilled about because the boss ordered them there. Often when I speak at leadership conferences, the audience wants to be there because they signed up and paid for it.

That said, you never know what's going on in people's lives. You may get an audience in which the majority happen to be having a bad day. Years ago, I spoke at a conference in Houston when Hurricane Ivan was on its way to Galveston. It was supposed to hit in the next twenty-four hours, so the whole audience was understandably distracted. People were on their phones and coming and going from the room the whole time. That time I understood what was going on, but sometimes you may not know why the audience is off. Here's how to deal with potentially difficult audiences:

- *Win over the audience before you begin.* Before your speech, go around the room and make small talk with people. Ask how they're doing, what traffic was like, and so on. This is a great way to get a feel for the mood of the room and know if it's going to be a tough crowd. It's easier to know beforehand and be ready for it than to realize it onstage. Sometimes I stand at the door and give people high fives or shake their hands as they enter, which helps build rapport with the audience before I ever set foot onstage. And if they do enter in a bad mood, this kind of thing may lift their spirits and actually put them in a better mood before you start speaking. You can tip the scale in your favor before you even start.
- *Ask the client about the audience.* They'll usually be honest with you and tell you if it's a difficult crowd. You can also ask the attendees, breaking the ice by saying something like, "Do you guys like coming to these things? How often do you do them? What are they usually like?"
- *Focus your time and energy on the people who want to be there.* Sometimes during the presentation I like to check on some goofball in the crowd who's not

paying attention, just to see if I've won him or her over. But some are going to be miserable no matter what. You cannot control them.

- *Don't ignore big distractions.* Occasionally someone is being so rude that it's a distraction to the entire audience and you need to address it. Let's say someone is talking on their phone. First, I like to make eye contact with the person. It's a nonverbal way of saying, "I see what you're doing. Knock it off." Sometimes, that alone is enough. If they see me and still don't get it, though, I may politely ask them, "Excuse me, sir? Could you do me a favor and stop talking on the phone? I think it's a distraction for those around you." Worst-case scenario: If that doesn't work, you can ask them to leave. Usually it won't come to that. After the situation is resolved, break the tension by making light of it, saying something like, "Well, that was fun."

If you handle these situations well, you'll gain further trust and respect from the audience, because trust and respect go both ways. You want them to trust you, but if you remove things that are negatively affecting their experience, they'll know you respect them as well. No matter what, if any of these situations happen and you end up with a tough audience, ask yourself what you could have done better. My mom used to say that if you're in a fight with someone and they are 99 percent wrong and you are 1 percent wrong, you still have room for improvement. Even if it's not your fault, there is something you can learn from and do better in almost every situation.

ACTION PLAN

1. Prepare a few activities to engage the audience ahead of time.

2. Think through some things that may go wrong and practice how you'd handle them.

3. Get to the venue early to gauge the audience before your talk.

> BONUS: Need help getting your audience involved and keeping them engaged in your presentation? Visit Speaker BookBonus.com.

9

What to Do after You're Done

The first thing you should do when you get offstage is take a deep breath and soak in the moment. You did it! You spent hours crafting and preparing a talk, and it all paid off. Be proud of what you've accomplished. Here's what to do next.

First, talk to as many audience members as possible. People will want to meet and talk with you, so give them that opportunity. Be fully present with them, as they just gave you the gift of their attention—honor that. Be aware of what's going on in the room. Maybe some people want to talk to you, but another session has started, in which case you should step out of the room. Also, make sure that you don't let one person monopolize your time. If you see a bunch of people gathered around you, thank the person you're speaking with and move on to the next person.

Then, thank the tech crew. These people make the event possible but are sadly overlooked by most people. You can make their day and impress the event planner by acknowledging and thanking them for their work. Also, return the mic, grab your laptop, and pick up anything you took onstage. If you're doing a workshop or seminar, leave the room better than you found it. Out of respect for the next speaker and for the venue, collect any extra worksheets lying around, straighten the chairs, and pick up any trash you see. These gestures not only are the right thing to do but they also help give you a reputation as a great person to work with.

After that, visit with the client to debrief. If they're right in the middle of something, you may have to do this later, but it's always good to check in with them at some point and ask how they thought it went and if they have any recommendations for you. If they're honest enough to give you some constructive criticism, that is incredibly valuable. Thank them for doing so, as it will likely make you better at what you do. When clients give you good feedback, ask if they'll write a recommendation letter or quote that you can use in your marketing. Getting them to make that verbal commitment while they're excited about you locks them in for when you follow up later.

And, of course, you'll want to thank them. They're very busy and have a lot going on, so overemphasize how much you appreciate them hiring and trusting you. I always give them a handwritten thank-you card. Speaking can be extremely draining, so after a speech I'll find a quiet place to gather my thoughts and decompress, maybe even grab a snack or a glass of water. Being onstage is a real high, and coming down from it can be exhausting, but it's important to me to always let the client know how grateful I am.

As soon as possible, make a list of what in your presentation worked and what needs improvement while all that information is still fresh in your mind. If the video of your presentation is available, be sure to review that at some point, taking note of which jokes landed, which stories connected, and what material fell flat. If you wait a week or two to do this, you may forget a lot of the nuances of what happened, so try to do this immediately.

When You Bomb . . .

Sometimes, though, the follow-up questions can result in disappointment. Early on in my career I delivered a presentation at a school assembly that, from my perspective, had gone really well.

Afterward I received a disappointing response from the principal in which she told me she wished I had focused more on the message and less on humor. After some thought I realized this was an assembly for seniors and the client had asked me to drive home a point that I hadn't. As I thought back through our pre-event call, I remembered her mentioning the topic she wanted me to focus on, thinking, "Yeah, sure, I'll touch on that," when really she wanted me to spend more time on it.

The whole experience didn't sit right with me, so I offered to send 250 more books to the school free of charge, in addition to the 100 I'd already sent, ensuring every single senior would get a copy of my book. This represented at least half of my speaking fee, but I wanted to do whatever was necessary to make it right with the client. The principal was thrilled, and we maintained a great relationship after that. I also learned a valuable lesson about managing and fulfilling expectations. Today, I am a lot more clear in my communication with the client about what I do and don't do, and I have that principal to thank.

That said, sometimes you just bomb, and no amount of effort can save you from the humiliation of failure. This can be depressing, and that's a totally normal way to feel. You're not alone and certainly not the exception. Every great speaker has bombed before; some have many times. This is how they became great. There have been more than a few times when partway through a presentation I've thought, "This is not going well, and I don't know how to get it back on track." If you haven't bombed yet, you will eventually, and you can use it to make yourself better.

As tough as crashing and burning can be, it's an opportunity to analyze yourself and reflect on what you could have done better. When you bomb, ask yourself the following questions:

- *Was it the environment?* Could everyone see and hear well? Were there distractions in the room? Did the technology work? I've been in settings where the talk and audience were fine, but because of the environment, I was set up to fail. The mic wasn't working or the room wasn't set up right or any number of other things went wrong. Again, this is why it's important to do everything you can beforehand to set yourself up for success. But sometimes there's nothing you can do.

WHAT TO DO AFTER YOU'RE DONE

- *Was it the audience?* What were they doing before and after the session? Were they tired? Did they ask questions? If you're doing a session the last day of a conference or right after lunch, it's going to affect how the attendees feel. They're going to be tired and want to go home.
- *Was it the talk itself?* Was the main objective clear? Were the stories and points interesting? Did it make sense and flow well? Was it all over the map and disjointed? Take a good look at it and dissect it to see if there is anything in it that can be improved.
- *Was it you?* Did you talk too slow or too fast? Did you not practice enough? Did you put energy into it? Did you feel confident? Did you deliver on what you promised? Were you glued to your slides? Did you give it your best?

If you really bomb, it's almost always a combination of a few factors. Often we are quick to point to the environment or audience or something outside of ourselves, but when reflecting on your talk, be brutally honest with yourself. You won't get better if you're not willing to own your part. Sometimes it's just you. Maybe you didn't bring 100 percent; maybe you weren't able. Maybe you were distracted due to some personal situation in your life. None of this means you're a bad speaker or a bad person. We all have off days. It just means you're human and that you may need to tweak a few things and be ready to do even better next time. Don't beat yourself up over it. Learn what you can from each gig, and they all have something to teach you—especially the failures. Then move on.

ACTION PLAN

1. Debrief with the client immediately after your talk. If they loved it, ask them for a recommendation.

2. Thank the event coordinator and everyone involved. To go above and beyond, send a follow-up thank-you note or card.

3. If you bombed, be honest about whether you gave it your best effort or if it was some outside factor. Learn from it and move on.

REVIEW: STEP 2

At this point you should have decided on your industry and topic, so it's time to create the talk. As we wrap up step 2, this is what you need to do next:

1. Pick what kind of talk you want to give: keynote, workshop, or seminar.

2. Develop an outline for that talk. While you may want to do multiple topics, just focus on one for now.

3. Write out the entire talk, word for word.

4. Practice, practice, practice. Practice your talk in front of someone else for bonus points.

WHAT TO DO AFTER YOU'RE DONE

Creating a great talk is the foundation for marketing and acquiring paid speaking gigs, which we'll cover later. Take your time here and make sure you're clear on your message, because it will matter later.

> BONUS: For more tips and resources on how to put together a great talk, visit SpeakerBookBonus.com.

Now let's move on to step 3.

STEP 3

ESTABLISH YOUR EXPERTISE

Once you've prepared a great talk, the next step in your journey down the Speaker Success Roadmap is establishing yourself as an expert. As a speaker, you want to be the go-to authority event planners consult to solve a specific problem for their audience. This is the problem you defined in step 1 and why we started there. Before you can start booking gigs, you have to define who you are, what you do, and who you do it for.

But just because you know something, that doesn't make you an expert in the eyes of others. What do you need, then? A brand. In this step, we're going to discuss branding and marketing, because it's not enough to know how to solve people's problems; they have to know you can do this for them. A brand is how other people tell your story. And marketing is the work you do to get that story out there.

Over the following few chapters, we'll help you define your brand as a speaker, identify the two most important marketing tools you need, and explain how to create them so that you establish your expertise and get the attention of a client.

10

Developing a Speaker Brand

When Kate Garnes went to her ten-year high school reunion, she felt depressed. In her hometown of Columbia, Missouri, she was the only one in her graduating class who didn't yet have a traditional job or wasn't married with kids. Despite the fact that it was her decision to take a nontraditional path in life, which included working at Walt Disney World and Universal Studios as a character performer, she was starting to feel the weight of that decision. Not to mention, those jobs weren't exactly bringing in the big bucks.

Kate had grown up tap-dancing and singing in the choir; she had always performed in one way or another. But the performance life was starting to weigh on her, and she realized she wasn't making the difference she wanted to make. At the reunion, she saw her peers living the kind of lives that made their parents proud, and that caused her to question her choices. Sitting at a picnic table feeling lost, she told an old friend how sad she felt, and the friend replied, "Well, what do you want to do with your life?"

Without missing a beat, Kate said, "I want to be a motivational speaker." Where that exactly came from, she wasn't sure, but on the flight back to Florida, Kate wrote eight letters to motivational speakers, asking their advice. "I have no idea what I'm doing," she told them, "but I *know* I'm supposed to do this." In little time, she heard back from five of them, and their responses were largely the same: do as much as you can to immerse yourself in everything related to speaking. So that's what she did.

Kate started consuming every piece of information on public speaking she could find, discovering *The Speaker Lab* podcast in the process. A few months later, she joined my Booked and Paid to Speak course, where she realized she wanted to work with high schoolers. She had always loved kids and didn't love speaking in front of adults, so choosing her industry was easy. In terms of speaking topic, her focus was on helping teens find worth in themselves when no one else was in their corner. "I like speaking to kids because high school is hard," she told me. "That's when you're figuring out who you are."

This desire to serve an audience came from an experience earlier in her life when Kate had a dance teacher who told her she wasn't going to make it as a dancer. This single experience had started a "record" playing in Kate's head that had continued for years, repeating the same message over and over that she would never be good enough. It took a long time for Kate to stop listening to that voice, but once she did, it changed everything.

DEVELOPING A SPEAKER BRAND

Once Kate got clear on her industry (speaking to teens), knew her interest (teaching self-worth), and had integrity (previous experience struggling with the same problem), it was time to immerse herself in training as a speaker. She flew to Memphis to work with a mentor on her talk, and in two intense days they mapped out the entire keynote she would start delivering. Now all that was left was the marketing. Kate had everything else she needed; now she just needed to get booked.

For many speakers, this is where the hard work begins. It's relatively easy to figure out who you want to speak to, what you want to speak about, and even how to develop a talk. It can be quite a challenge, though, to sell yourself. Many people struggle to grasp that *they* are the product, and this was especially difficult for Kate. She had to get other people to see her as *the* authority, which is no small thing for a young woman who had struggled for much of her life with feeling good enough.

Before she could book a gig, she needed a brand. Remember that a brand is a story other people tell about you. So how do you get them to tell that story?

Kate created a one-page website and a basic demo video showcasing her talents, which she filmed in an empty theater a friend at Walt Disney World let her use. There was no one in the audience and her friend filmed it on her iPhone, but it was enough. Another friend who knew a little about video editing offered to help with the project, and together they edited the video on their phones. "And it was awful," Kate recalled. "But it got the job done!" The next year, she booked fifteen speaking gigs, including three national conferences—all done in less than a year and with nothing other than a simple website and a homemade demo video.

Establishing yourself as an expert isn't hard. It's a process anyone can learn, but you have to be willing to do the work and get creative. When clients come to your site, you need to show them your best, which means you have to do your best to represent yourself. The good news is, you have more resources than you realize, maybe even some good friends, as Kate did, who can help you get the word out.

You Are the Brand

Maybe you don't like the idea that you are a brand or that you have to market yourself, but this is something every professional communicator does, and you will have to do the same. Whether you realize it or not, you're communicating something about what you do, so in a sense, you already have a brand. The real work now is just to make it stronger.

The most important lesson you as a speaker can learn about developing your brand is that your company is not the brand. Your teaching is not the brand. Your product is not the brand. *You* are the brand. This is the most fundamental part of positioning yourself as an expert. Take me, for example: Nobody has any idea what my legal company name is. I own grantbaldwin.com, which is my speaking website, and I run TheSpeakerLab.com, where I offer training programs for speakers, but nobody has any idea what my legal business name is, because it doesn't matter. When clients book me to speak, they're booking Grant Baldwin. When students buy my courses or come to my retreats, they're looking to learn directly from me, not my company. My legal company name is The Baldwin Group, but I'm the face of everything. I'm the brand. So are you.

If you don't have a company name, this should be easy. But if you do, it's normal for this to be a little uncomfortable. A lot of my clients, even the ones with corporate backgrounds who have been selling products for years, struggle to sell themselves. It's a real shift. But if you don't do this in an industry where the individual is the brand, your business and message will suffer. You have only one shot to make a first impression. Potential clients will make assumptions about you as a speaker based on your marketing materials, which means that bad marketing will make you look like a bad speaker.

Your brand is what you communicate, and you are always communicating something with everything you say and with what you don't. The goal, then, is to be as clear as possible. Branding is not so much about beauty as it is about clarity. Certainly, it's important to have an attractive website and a cool-looking demo video, but more than that, you need a brand that is clear.

In Kate's case, she teaches young people how to believe in themselves and have confidence. That's simple and clear and something just about anyone can grasp. That's a brand.

Everything You Do Is Marketing

So what is a brand? Is it a logo? A website? A video?

Well, yes, it can include those things, but it's much more than that. Your brand is the feeling you give your clients; it's the story they tell themselves before, during, and after they buy your product or service. It's that feeling of reassurance they get when they see you onstage, killing it.

Think about the different products we buy. Why is it that some of us buy brand-name products instead of generic products, even though the quality may be the same, and others avoid brand names altogether? Is it because some of us think brand names are higher quality and others consider ourselves sensible shoppers? Who's right, and who's wrong? It depends on the story you tell yourself.

Similarly, when Apple fans buy a MacBook or an iPhone, paying two to three times the cost of what a competitor would charge, they're telling themselves a story, usually something like, "This is worth it." When you drive a hybrid car and remind yourself that you care about the environment, that's a story as well. It's all branding. From the environment we create for our customers to the way we deliver our message to the stories we help our customers tell themselves, everything we do is marketing.

The same is true for you and the brand you're building as a speaker. What is your ideal client looking for? How can you best illustrate that through your website, demo video, and other communication? How can you reinforce what you communicated after they hire you? What extra thoughtful gesture can you do to stand out from other speakers in your industry and reinforce the brand you're trying to build?

We discussed in a previous chapter texting your client when you arrive at an event and following up with them via a personal email or handwritten note—this is all part of the brand, the story you're telling. If you tell it well, others will start telling it for you, and that's how you build a brand.

Let's now look at how to do this, practically, without taking out an extra mortgage.

Branding Yourself without Breaking the Bank

Although it's important that your website and marketing materials look great, you don't have to spend a lot of money up front to make them professional. And with all the great tools out there today, you don't need to spend a lot of time either.

I tend to be as resourceful as possible, finding ways to bootstrap my way to success wherever I can. I don't believe in going into debt, and when I was starting out as a speaker, I figured out ways to do things myself or bartered with others to get it done. Branding, however, is one area where you don't want to skimp if at all possible. I'm not saying go broke getting a good-looking website, but just be careful about being too cheap. If your branding is careless, it communicates that you are a careless speaker. That may not be accurate, but that's the way the client will see it.

As a new speaker, you don't need a lot of fancy marketing materials or strategies. You don't need to pay to advertise your services or spend tens of thousands of dollars on a campaign to get your message out there. But you do need to spend some time developing a great brand, because event planners will judge you within seconds of seeing your site and video. And you definitely need two important marketing assets: a website and a speaker reel.

So how do we begin?

First, consider your network. Is there anyone you could barter with to help you build a website or create a video? A couple of years ago our Christmas card looked like a professional photo shoot, but my sister shot it on her iPhone. Recently I paid a friend $75 to shoot some promotional photos.

ESTABLISH YOUR EXPERTISE

My current demo video was shot by a guy who has done videos for Tony Robbins, Richard Branson, and Tim Ferriss. He's very expensive, but he shot it for free in exchange for some coaching. You may not be able to offer coaching, but my point is, there are ways to make something look great for very little money. I'm almost certain you have skills to offer in exchange for someone in your network to help you with your marketing.

Before you spend any money, ask around and see if you have any family or friends who do design work. You can ask friends for referrals, text or call a few people you know, or even put it out there on social media. There may be someone in your network who has skills you never knew about or maybe knows someone with whom you can exchange services. Maybe that person is just getting started and looking to build his or her portfolio. Another route is to contact a local university or community college with a graphic design program and see if there are any students looking for work. They are most likely cheaper than professionals but can still be quite talented. The point is, you can get quality on a budget; you don't have to break the bank to build a great brand. There are some really great resources and websites that offer less expensive website and design work, which we'll discuss in chapter 12.

It's important when you're creating a design and a look for your business to have a consistent brand. Anything you send out should have the same look and feel. Your website, demo video, and any marketing materials should not have totally different designs. This means using a simple and consistent color scheme, the same kind of fonts, etc. The more cluttered your stuff is, the more confusing your message will be, and the less interested potential clients will be.

DEVELOPING A SPEAKER BRAND

That said, don't be too hard on yourself. We all start somewhere, but as you saw with Kate's story, it doesn't take much to begin. My first speaker reel was horrible, but it was the best I could pull off at the time. My website has improved a lot over the years as well. Today, I have a much better video and a great site, but only because I used what I had, booked some gigs, got paid, and reinvested some of that money back into my marketing. A brand is something you are continually growing as you go further down the path of becoming a successful speaker. Remember that no matter what you do, you are communicating something about the kind of work you do, and that's your brand. Do what you can with what you have, and keep making it better. Over the next couple of chapters, we'll get into the nitty-gritty on how to make your marketing assets as good as possible.

ACTION PLAN

1. Think through your brand. What are your potential clients looking for? What kind of story do you want them to tell about you?

2. Ask your community for help. Ask around and see if you have friends or family members with photography, website, or video skills.

> BONUS: For more help developing your speaker brand, visit SpeakerBookBonus.com.

11

Getting a Great Demo Video

Your demo video is the most important part of your website, and aside from having a great talk, it's the best piece of marketing you will ever have.

When a nightclub hires a band, the first thing they do is go listen to the band's music. As the owner of a club, you would never hire a band without hearing them first. The same is true for speaking. Event planners don't want to be told what a great speaker you are; they want to see it for themselves. So let's help you create a great video that will get you booked and paid to speak.

But what if you don't have any footage yet? How can you create a speaker reel if you don't have any video of you speaking? This is a common question I get from students and clients all the time. You have a few options.

GETTING A GREAT DEMO VIDEO

First, you can find a local event where you can speak for free, just for the purpose of getting the footage. My first video was mostly me speaking to a local church youth group. You could speak at a Rotary Club, a chamber of commerce, Toastmasters, meetings at work, church, etc. All of these are free options. Get creative.

The second thing you can do is host your own event. It doesn't have to be fancy. You could just rent a room at a coffee shop, library, or restaurant and invite friends and family to come. Even just five or ten people would be enough of an audience to hear reactions and even test out some material.

The last and least preferable option is to speak to an empty room. It's not preferable because it's hard as a speaker to bring your A game and speak with energy to an empty room. But I've seen people do it and make it work. For a first-time speaker, it's a perfectly fine option. Just don't add anything fake like laugh tracks.

If you're not a tech-savvy person, the easiest way to edit your video is to outsource it. There are plenty of affordable options available in terms of individuals you can hire or services you can use. If you are tech savvy, however, or just want to give it a try yourself, there are plenty of great tools you can use as well.

You want your video up and website ready before you start marketing yourself so that you have something to show your potential clients.

Gear You May Need

When it comes to cameras, one of the best cameras that you can use is your phone. These days they have amazing capabilities, and if you're filming your demo video or taking photos yourself, it's a pretty good option. If you have a friend who has a fancy camera, or if you can afford a professional videographer, then by all means do that. Using your phone is a perfectly good option, though. I shoot a lot of video on my iPhone, and it works great.

For microphones, there are a handful of affordable lavalier mics that you can clip onto your shirt and from which you can run a cord to your phone or camera. This is a great DIY option. One trick I learned from a professional videographer is to use two iPhones: one with the lavalier mic hooked up to it so it's recording audio and one offstage with a trusted friend to capture the room and you speaking. You don't want to depend on the audio being picked up from the camera that's shooting video because often it's going to pick up ambient sound and not be great quality. It's going to catch people moving around, paper shuffling, etc. You really want to have a nice mic on you recording audio for your demo video. You can sync the audio from one iPhone and the video from the other in editing.

If you're really strapped for cash, you can even just use the voice memo or camera app on your phone. It's not as great, but it will work.

Making Your Demo Video

Once you have some video of you speaking, here are eight tips for making a high-quality demo video.

1. *Keep it short.* Consider your own attention span for online video. Twelve minutes in online video land is

like an eternity. Your video should be no more than three to five minutes.
2. *Think of it as a movie trailer.* Trailers take a two-hour movie and boil it down to two minutes so you know the basic plot, theme, and cast. Your demo video should be short enough that they get an overview but leave them wanting more. It's a reflection of your entire talk. If you use a lot of humor in your presentations, include some jokes. If your talk is about your life story, show some pieces of that. Don't be afraid to include your best material in your video.
3. *Show, don't tell.* The video should be you actually speaking, not you talking about speaking. Sometimes speakers use highlight reels of media clips and interviews with maybe a voice over about how great they are, but that's not what clients want to see. They want to see you speaking.
4. *Include your contact info and website throughout the video.* If someone finds you through YouTube or somewhere else, you want it to be easy for them to connect with you.
5. *When necessary, offer context.* Often, you can't tell from a video how many people are in the room or who you're talking to, what the environment is like, etc. It may be necessary to tell them with a quick slide at the beginning saying you are speaking to an audience of two hundred at their annual sales meeting. Keep this in mind when showing stories or jokes. If you tell a five-minute story with a big punchline that gets a great laugh, it won't have the same

effect on someone watching your demo video if they haven't heard the entire joke. Try to include the setup to the joke as well, not just the punch line.

6. *Skip the bells and whistles.* New speakers sometimes assume they need to have a professionally produced video to get hired. But that's not true. Most clients don't need to see that. I edited my first demo video myself with Windows Movie Maker and had plenty of success with that video. Just keep it clean and simple. You've heard me say it before: start with what you've got and improve as you go along.

7. *Make sure the link to the demo video is in a prominent place, like at the top of the page.* The main thing you want website visitors to do is press play on that video, so it should be hard to miss.

8. *Make sure it's mobile friendly.* Most websites and emails are viewed on phones or tablets these days, so you want it to be easy for potential clients if they're not viewing it on a computer.

ACTION PLAN

1. Decide how, when, and where you will shoot your demo video.

2. Shoot it. Whether you DIY, hire someone, or have a friend do it, just make sure it gets done. It won't be your demo video forever, so don't get hung up on it not being perfect.

BONUS: Go to SpeakerBookBonus.com for a list of recommended mics, video equipment, tools, and resources, including the best tools to use for filming and editing on any budget.

12

Setting Up Your Speaker Website

Your website is the first place many potential clients will land when they research you, so it's a critical part of establishing yourself as the expert. It is also an important marketing tool and a big part of your brand, so it needs to be professional and sharp.

A lot of people, however, put a lot of unnecessary information on their website that ends up confusing the client. Remember the goal of a brand is clarity. In this chapter, we'll focus on the essentials of what makes a great speaker website and how you can get started creating that today.

The first step is to determine the goals of your website and who it is for. Just as in step 1 when you selected a problem to solve for a specific audience, your website isn't for everyone. That's why getting clear on who you want to speak to has

SETTING UP YOUR SPEAKER WEBSITE

to come first. It's the foundation of everything and affects every part of this process.

Many speakers make the mistake of thinking their website should be geared toward their audience. It shouldn't. Your website needs to speak directly to those who are looking to hire you as a speaker, which may not necessarily be your audience.

When I first started, I was speaking to a lot of high school students, but the high school students weren't the ones hiring me. I was usually being hired by forty- or fifty-year-old school administrators, so my website needed to be targeted at them, not the students. If you speak to churches or youth groups, it's not a member of the congregation who is hiring you, but more often it is the pastor. Think through who the decision makers are in your niche, and build your website with them in mind. They're your audience, at least the first people you're going to have to impress.

Once we know who the audience is, we can get started building our simple website.

Your Simple, One-Page Website

All you need to get started as a speaker is a simple, one-page website with two main goals: first, to get people to watch your demo video, and second, to get them to contact you.

As you build your website, consider what clients want to see on a website that will give them confidence in you. Browse other speakers' websites and speakers' bureau pages, taking note of what you like and don't like. After you've done some research and thought through what you want to communicate, here are the six essential elements of a simple speaker website:

1. *Demo video.* Your demo video should be in a prominent position on the website, ideally at the top of the page and practically impossible to miss.
2. *Contact info.* Below the video, make it clear what the next step is with a "call to action" button or a form for them to fill out once they've watched the video. Often you'll see language like "book me" or "hire me," but try to keep it more casual with something like "check my availability" or "learn more." You want a low barrier to entry so that you can start a conversation with them. Like a first date, you're just getting to know each other with no commitment necessary right now. If someone has more questions or wants to book you, make it easy for them. Including both a phone number and email is ideal. You can list these in a couple places on your website in addition to having a form they can fill out that goes to your email inbox.
3. *Pictures.* You can use these anywhere throughout your website, but be sure to include both speaking and normal life photos. The speaking ones help you look professional to potential clients, and the normal life pictures let people get to know you a bit. Remember: you are the brand, and people do business with people they know, like, and trust. I have some speaking pictures beside my demo video and some normal life pictures in my "about" section (you can see these at SpeakerBookBonus.com).

4. *Recommendations.* You can request recommendations from anyone who has heard you speak. Of course, it's good to have testimonials from event planners and authorities in your industry, but if you don't have those, just get some from anyone who has nice things to say about your speaking. In the future, make it a habit to always ask for a few testimonials after each gig. We'll go deeper into this in the next part, but for now, use the testimonials you have and always ask for more. Once you've acquired these, be sure to list the client you worked with and where you spoke under the quote. A word of warning, though: be ethical. A speaker spoke at an event hosted by a prestigious university, which had nothing to do with the event other than the event planner had rented a room there. On the speaker's website, he had listed that he'd spoken at that school, which the school noticed and asked him to remove. Remember that having integrity is part of becoming a successful speaker. Only list clients who have directly hired you to speak, and don't fudge it to make yourself seem more credible. Also, don't downplay it. I once spoke at State Farm Insurance at their headquarters in Illinois, where they hired me to speak to about a hundred interns in a specific department. Was I speaking to the whole company or a bunch of top executives? No. But State Farm's national headquarters hired me, so that's something I include on my website.

5. *Bio.* Clients want to know who you are and why you do what you do. You may want to include a few random facts or funny stories about yourself if it fits

your personality. This all comes down to what your brand is and how you want people to think of you. For many clients, it will be the things that make you human that will distinguish you from other speakers, so don't be afraid to include a few things like that in the bio section of your website.
6. *Topics.* This goes back to the menu metaphor we used earlier. This is a list of speaking options that you offer clients, including the types of events and recommended audiences each talk works best for. You know your material better than anyone; you know which talk is a good fit for which audience, so let them know.

It's okay to have more than one page on your website. You may want to include a page for your blog or podcast if you have one. Some speakers have a resource page, calendar, or even online store where they sell products. Keep in mind, though, that every page you add will take away from the main actions you want the client to take, which is to watch your video and reach out to you.

Some speakers like to have an "opt-in" or a place to collect email addresses. This works if you have an idea of how you want to grow your speaking business beyond the scope of speaking, but it's not absolutely necessary at the beginning. That said, if you can collect email addresses for your list, I always recommend doing so, because you can leverage that influence in other ways down the line. Just remember that your email list will likely be buyers or customers of your other services and products, not necessarily people hiring you for speaking gigs.

How to Do It Yourself

If you have the ability to hire someone to set up your website, that's great. If not, you can do it yourself. Here's how:

- *Choose a domain name.* If possible, just use your name, like GrantBaldwin.com, for example. Try to get a .com domain if you can, which is typically regarded as the most authoritative domain and the most common. If your name is too difficult to spell or you can't get your actual name, pick something that is simple and easy to spell. Remember, you are the brand, so the domain should be about you, not your company or message.
- *Get a personalized email address.* This also contributes to the brand you're building. Lisa@lisasmith.com is much stronger than Lisa1234@hotmail.com. You can usually set this up with your web host.
- *Decide where to build your website.* If you are a little more tech savvy and want your website to look exactly a certain way, go with WordPress. If not, Squarespace is easier to set up with lots of drag-and-drop features.
- *Get a good design.* Even if you're on a budget, you still want to get as high-quality a website design as you can. When you're just getting started, you may not have a lot of money to spend on a website or marketing, and that's okay. There are affordable themes available on both WordPress and Squarespace that make this fairly easy. Design is always going to be important to your brand.

Social Media

Social media is not nearly as important as your website and demo video, especially when you're just starting, but it's helpful to have a presence in at least one or two channels where people in your industry are connecting. So if you're targeting corporate audiences, you may choose to focus on LinkedIn instead of Twitter, or if you want to speak at parenting conferences, it may be that Facebook is a better place to plant your digital flag. The point is that it's better to be intentional than to try to be everywhere online.

Remember Dr. Sue, the veterinarian who speaks on pet cancer? In 2011 she published a book called *The Dog Cancer Survival Guide*. As the book was coming out, a friend, who was also a social media expert, recommended she buy drsuecancervet.com and get on social media. "What would I do with that?" she thought. But she did it anyway. Slowly, it grew over time until one day she shared a post on Facebook of a story about a golden retriever who had lost his leg to cancer and was celebrating his birthday. People loved the story and started sharing it, which caused her to realize there was a real need for people to learn about pet cancer with a voice of optimism. Setting up her website helped a lot of people learn more about her. She was one of very few veterinarians who had an established brand, and it helped her stand out. Now she has 35,000 fans on Facebook and a private group of over 2,700 veterinary professionals.

Social media can be powerful, but it should be used as part of a bigger marketing plan to get people to your website and watch your demo video so they can book you. If it feels too overwhelming for you right now, just focus on your website and video. Your website is the digital home for your brand, which will help establish you as an expert in your industry, so make sure you take your time and do it right, understanding that you can continue to tweak it as you go.

ACTION PLAN

1. Do your research. Look at other speakers' websites and decide what you like and don't like.

2. Pick your domain name, hosting, and personalized email address. You're the real deal now.

3. Create a simple one-page website, following the tips in this chapter.

4. Set up your social media accounts. Pick just one to focus on for now.

REVIEW: STEP 3

To be a successful speaker, you need to look and act like one. Here's a review of what we just covered to establish yourself as an expert:

1. Understand that you are the brand.

2. Record your demo video.

3. Create a personalized email address that accurately reflects your brand.

4. Build a simple one-page website.

> BONUS: To see a list of resources that can help with finding the right hosting, domain, and design for your website, along with resources and tutorials on how to build your website, go to SpeakerBookBonus.com.

Now that you've got all your essential marketing materials and are building that brand that is you, let's move on to step 4 so that we can start getting you booked and paid to speak.

STEP 4
ACQUIRE PAID SPEAKING GIGS

Now the fun begins. Everything we've done thus far has been laying the foundation for your speaking career, including figuring out your industry and interest, honing your message, and even getting your website and video up. Now it's time to start putting the finishing touches on this new career you're creating. In other words, it's time to get some speaking gigs.

This is where a lot of speakers make a crucial mistake, thinking, "Well, I've got my website online and my speaker video up, so I'm done." But your phone isn't going to start ringing just because you have a website; your inbox isn't going to be flooded with speaking requests now that you've finished your speaker video. In many ways, the work is just beginning. Now your job is to identify potential clients and reach out to them to find out if they need a speaker for their upcoming event. If you're lucky, some people may find you through your website; certainly, that happens on occasion—in fact, the longer you speak, the more it may happen—but the quickest way to start booking gigs is to ask for them.

But where and how?

That's what step 4, Acquire Paid Speaking Gigs, is all about. No one will care more about helping you get speaking gigs than you, so let's help you figure out how to start wearing the hat of "speaking agent" so you can get out there and start speaking.

13

Finding Paid Speaking Gigs

Four days into his senior year of college, Pete Smith made a dramatic shift with the trajectory of his life. About to graduate with a degree in political science, he informed his parents that he would not be attending law school as previously planned and instead would become a professional speaker, to which his dad replied, "What on earth will you speak about and who will listen?"

Pete later admitted that his father had a point. "I was twenty-one and had no life experience," he said. After college, Pete didn't end up pursuing speaking as he had declared to his parents and, perhaps to the satisfaction of his father, took a job in landscape design. Later, Pete became a high school history teacher and continued working in education and then operations until the age of thirty-five, when he had a stroke. During the stroke, he had a startling vision, a sixty-second flash of insight, which served as a reminder that he would not live forever. "It wasn't like my life flashed before my eyes," he said, "it was about significance. I wondered if I mattered. Society continues to tell us that happiness and success are what matters, but all I thought about were fulfillment and significance."

After the stroke, Pete quit his job and began taking life into his own hands. Using his previous work experience, he kept himself and his family financially afloat by doing whatever consulting and training gigs he could drum up. In 2014 he was invited to speak at a local Rotary Club. In previous jobs, Pete had done a bit of speaking but hadn't thought about it much since that day he talked to his dad. Usually, he would have done a talk on leadership, but instead he decided for some reason to speak about his stroke and the lessons it had taught him. The speech struck a nerve with the audience in such a profound way that Pete decided to give speaking another shot.

After taking our Booked and Paid to Speak course, Pete booked five paid gigs in his first year. The next year, he booked twenty; the year after that, thirty-one; then forty-two. Today, 80 to 90 percent of Pete's income is solely from speaking. How does he do it? He asks to speak. He doesn't wait for the speaking gigs to come to him; he goes out and finds them. And he is not alone in his tenacity. Most professional speakers I know built their careers by finding the right gigs for themselves and asking to speak.

In the case of Pete, he is particularly driven. He's a proposal machine, sending out three to four hundred requests a year. "Everyone always says, 'Work smarter, not harder,'" he remarked. "But at first you have to learn how to work smarter." And one of the ways to do that is to simply work harder until you learn what works and what doesn't. Even so, there's something to be said for simply putting the hours in. Pete is an established speaker who earns an average of $9,950 per speech plus travel, and still he cranks out hundreds of proposals per year. "I don't know why no one else does it," he told me.

A mentor once told him, "Speakers never retire, the phone just stops ringing." Pete is determined to keep that from happening. You can do the same; it's actually quite simple. All you have to do is pick up the phone, dust off the laptop, and start reaching out. If you want to get booked and keep getting booked, you just have to learn how to ask, and that's what we're going to focus on for the rest of this section. But first, I want to share with you some of the best strategies for finding paid speaking gigs and how to utilize them.

Google: The First Place You Should Go

Do you want to know one of the best ways to find speaking gigs without having an inside person? Just google it. You would not believe how many gigs I have gotten and how many my training clients have found simply by searching online for "_____ conference" (fill in the blank with your industry).

Online search engines like Google and Bing are a great way to find events that need speakers—and these tools are, of course, completely free to use. For example, let's say you speak on dog training. You search phrases like "dog training conference," "dog training association," "dog trainer conference," or even "dog trainer event." Then you can add your state, region, province, and territory to the search. State and regional events are generally great places to get started because they're smaller, lower risk, and have lower budgets, so they don't tend to target national speakers. At this point, this is actually good for you, because it means you have a shot at getting booked. These smaller events are often looking for more of an up-and-coming speaker, which means *you*.

If you already have some speaking experience, think about a recent event you spoke at that you enjoyed and then search for other events similar to it. For example, maybe it was an HR event you really enjoyed. Well, of course, there are other HR departments you could speak to, including at local, regional, and national conferences. There may even be other departments similar to HR that have their own events, and maybe you would be qualified to speak to them as well. Brainstorm where these people gather and start targeting those events.

The biggest investment when you start searching for places to speak will be your time. It takes a lot of time to search terms and go through all the results, which you could potentially outsource, but it's not something I recommend. Why? Because your goal is to build a relationship, and the more familiar you are with the client and their industry, company, or events, the better you can serve them. When you can show that you know them and are genuinely interested in serving them, they will trust you. If you don't do this legwork yourself, you'll miss out on being able to target your content and communication specifically for them and lower your chances of getting booked.

SEO: Let Them Come to You

When using any search engine, there is a technique called search engine optimization (SEO), which we won't go into deeply, but it's good to know the basics because this is a good long-term strategy for you to be found by new clients. Here are a few basic tips on how to get started with SEO:

- *Pick a keyword or phrase.* Think through what people who are looking for a speaker like you would search for. If you speak to high school students, they may search for "youth speaker," "teen speaker," "youth motivational speaker," "high school speaker," or maybe "youth leadership speaker." Those are all examples of keyword phrases.
- *Consider the variations of that same phrase.* Think about the different ways they might search for you online. For your site to be "optimized" for these terms means there's a good chance someone will find you through search engines. It means you'll land high up in the search results.
- *Get as specific as you can.* Something like "sales speaker" or "customer service speaker" are going to have a lot of searches and will be hard to rank for. Think about some nontraditional, less common variations of search terms such as "manufacturing sales speaker in Nashville."

Once you've identified some key terms and phrases, you can start creating content using these terms and phrases so that people can find you online. The words you use online in describing what you do will help get the attention of search engines, which will allow other people to find you. SEO is a lot more involved than that, but this is a good way to get your content out there and to just get started. You can google "search engine optimization" to get a better idea of how it works.

Client Referrals: Ask and You Shall Receive

After you speak somewhere, *always* ask the event planner for other contacts who book similar speakers. This is the best way to get future gigs. Nothing means more to people than a recommendation from a trusted friend. Think about it: If you're buying a product, are you more likely to buy it when someone you don't know pitches it to you or when a friend says, "Hey, you should try this, it's great!"? The latter obviously carries a lot more weight.

After a gig has gone well, ask the client, "Do you know other event planners or conferences that may be looking for a speaker similar to me?" If you've done a good job, they will almost always recommend you to their peers—and not just out of the goodness of their heart, but also because it makes them look more credible to their peers when they make good recommendations.

As I shared in the previous chapter, it's also a good idea to ask for client testimonials, which you can use to reach out to future clients. You get bonus points if you can get letters of recommendation on the client's letterhead (see examples of great client recommendation letters at SpeakerBookBonus.com). One way to do this is by asking up front in your negotiations with the client. Include a request in your contract that if the client is satisfied with your work they will write a letter of recommendation. I've used this before both in contracts and when negotiating my fee. If for some reason the client can't pay your full fee, you can offer to reduce it a bit in return for recommendations or introductions to other clients. Sometimes, this is even more valuable than getting paid your full fee.

For clients who don't write a letter, you can put together a letter based on their verbal feedback and send it to them for approval, which is much easier for the client. There will likely be an opportunity for you to get their feedback right after your talk. Often when you get offstage, the client will say several things about how great you were, and that's the perfect opportunity to say, "Hey, do you mind if I put some of those things you just said together in a letter from you to send to other clients? I'll send it to you first so you can make sure it represents how you feel." That takes all the work out of their hands and is an easy "yes" for them.

When you get a recommendation letter from a client, ask them, if at all possible, to send it to their contacts themselves, as this will be more well received than if you were to send it. If you reach out to an event planner and say, "Hey, my friend Susie told me to talk to you," that's one thing. But if someone else writes to that event planner and says, "Hey, you need to talk to my friend Grant," that is a lot more effective, especially if they already know each other.

Pay-per-Click: A Little More Advanced

A more advanced strategy is to pay for advertising through pay-per-click services such as Google or Facebook, where you pay a small fee for each person who clicks on your ad.

Typically, this requires a low investment with a potentially high return. For example, if you spend $100 on ads per month and only fifty people come to your site, but two of them book you for a $2,000 gig, then that's a huge return on your investment. Even one gig would be great. Typically, for these services there's no minimum you have to spend, so you can spend as much or as little as you want, even a few dollars. It's a low-risk way to dip your toe into paid advertising if you're looking to do that.

The more specific you can be in terms of the keywords you're targeting in your ads, the better. Vague keywords such as "motivational speaker" are usually more expensive because there are going to be a lot of people competing for that search term. Ads targeting broad, common keywords are going to cost you more per click because they theoretically have more value. For example, "medical industry customer service speaker" is a very specific and not competitive keyword, so you may only pay a few cents for something like that, which is way better than "customer service speaker." There may not be a lot of people searching for "medical industry customer service speaker" because it's so niche-specific, but if they do, you'll definitely be toward the top of the results. So try to think as specifically as possible.

With pay-per-click, make sure you run tests to see what works. Test out different keywords with small dollar amounts. You may also consider video ads on other platforms or even hire a virtual assistant to help you figure out video on other platforms.

One way to take it to the next level is to create landing pages for your most popular search terms so that when someone clicks on your ad, they land on the page that you've created for someone searching that term, instead of just taking them to your homepage. If you're targeting the "medical industry customer service speaker" keyword, you can have a landing page specifically for event planners in that industry. This approach creates a more personal touch and makes them think you are exactly what they're looking for. If you're just starting out, though, and experimenting with ads, it's perfectly fine to send them to your homepage or demo video.

Before you run these ads, you need to make sure that everything we covered in step 3 about your website and demo video are completely ready. Of course, this strategy can be very time intensive and requires a level of technical understanding that some will not want to spend the time developing. But it is still a useful strategy.

Speaker Referrals: What Goes Around Comes Around

In my first full year of speaking, my largest source of business was referrals from other speakers. Building relationships with other professionals in your niche is an important and effective referral strategy and can be done no matter how long you've been at it. Even though you may technically be competitors, most speakers are extremely friendly and willing to help you, especially when you're just getting started. Everyone started from scratch; some speakers are just a little further down the road than others. If you get out there and start attending conferences and industry events, you should be able to begin building connections with other speakers, many of whom may be willing to help.

But why would a speaker refer business to you when they could just take the gig themselves? Speakers refer clients to other speakers in several different situations:

- Because the budget for the event is too low and they can't afford a certain speaker. If someone is a $5,000 speaker but the speaking budget for an event is $1,000, they may refer to you if your fee is less.
- Because they are already booked on a certain date. The same logic applies: it's better for their relationship with the client for the speaker to decline and refer someone else than to just decline.
- Because it's not a topic they speak on. If someone reaches out to me and wants me to speak on customer service but I don't know much about that, I can refer them to a friend of mine who does.
- Because some speakers don't want to travel very far. Or perhaps I know someone local to an event who could speak and cut down on travel costs.

I'm happy to refer other speakers, especially after I've done a great job and the event organizer wants recommendations on who else is an outstanding speaker. This is a relationship business, so building and maintaining rapport with your fellow speakers is important.

This is not as selfless as it may seem. Referring business to another speaker reflects well on the speaker who gives the referral. For example, if the client doesn't have the budget for your friend but can afford you, it's better for your friend to say, "I can't do it, but I can recommend a friend of mine

FINDING PAID SPEAKING GIGS

who may be able to," rather than, "I can't do it; you don't have enough money." You can be that speaker's plan B—a secret weapon, so to speak. And if you do a great job, that makes your friend look good too.

Speakers rarely refer other speakers if they haven't heard them speak before. To some extent, their reputation is on the line too. If you refer a speaker and they do a bad job, you have most likely burned a bridge with the client. So if someone does refer you, understand that means they trust you, and you shouldn't take that lightly. Again, this is another reason why you have to get out there and start speaking, so other speakers can see you and be able to refer you to clients.

One word of caution, though: Never send a cold email to a speaker you respect and ask them to refer you for a gig. If they don't know you and aren't confident in your skills, they won't do it, and you'll probably damage a potential relationship with them by asking too soon. And if you ever recommend other speakers, make sure you let them know you did, because they will want to follow up with the client themselves. It also just builds goodwill between you. Even if they don't end up booking the gig, it's an honor to be referred, and such a gesture shows you're out there speaking to clients about them. Again, this isn't completely selfless, as it may incentivize others to do the same for you. But, of course, don't do it for that reason; do it because you want to refer them, not because you're expecting them to "owe you."

Depending on the relationship, occasionally another speaker may ask for a commission for the referral, meaning if you ask another speaker to refer you, and you get paid for the gig, it's sometimes expected that you will pay that person a percentage of what you earned from the gig, usually around 10 percent of whatever the client paid you. If it's a good friend, I typically don't ask for anything because we're friends, and I trust they would do the same for me.

Showcases

Showcases are basically auditions for speakers and are most common in the college and conference markets. Depending on the event, either they will do live auditions or you may submit your talk idea online. In the case of the college market, typically five to ten speakers audition live, and each speaks for fifteen to twenty minutes. The audience is made up of decision makers considering whom to hire. If you're interested in speaking to the college market, I encourage you to check out associations that offer showcases, such as the National Association for Campus Activities and the Association for the Promotion of Campus Activities.

There are, of course, pros and cons to this strategy. The pro is that there are a lot of people in the room who want to hire speakers, so you have a decent chance of getting booked, and it offers great exposure. The con is that you are one of many they are considering, so competition is fierce. It can be difficult to know how to differentiate yourself from others, but this is yet another reason why you should have a great talk that is polished and ready to go.

Sometimes conferences have an open call for speaking submissions. This can be a great way to get considered for a speaking gig. Most conferences that offer speaking submissions tell you exactly how to submit on their website. These are often for workshops, not always keynotes, so be aware of that going in. Sometimes the audience votes; more often than not, it's the event planning staff who decides. But each event has its own way of doing things, so just read the instructions online to be aware of the guidelines. Even if it's a smaller speaking gig, an unpaid workshop, or an opportunity to get your conference fee waived, this can be a great opportunity to get your foot in the door.

Media and Press

Sometimes organizations and groups aren't looking just for a speaker. They're looking for an expert who happens to speak on a specific topic. A good question to ask yourself is, "What websites, blogs, or publications do my decision makers read?" Then ask yourself, "How can I put my name in front of them as an authority and go-to figure?" A good resource is HARO (Help a Reporter Out), a free resource journalists use to look for sources on specific topics. If you get on their email list, they send multiple emails a day about reporters looking for insights and feedback on a given subject. Getting featured in a place where your target audience and decision makers will see you can increase your bookings and credibility as an expert.

Remember, this is a numbers game. The more potential clients you can find, the more outreach you do, the more likely you are to get some yeses. Over time this will come more naturally, and you may even start thinking, "Where do these people gather? What are their conferences? What are their events? Where are their trade shows? What are their industry associations?" The deeper you get into acquiring paid speaking gigs, the more ideas will follow. Just start looking. Connect with other speakers and event planners and start proactively building relationships. Once you start doing that, you can dive more deeply into identifying and contacting decision makers. But it starts here first, with doing the legwork to find out where those decision makers may be and reaching out.

Before Reaching Out

In the following chapter, we will talk more about how to make the ask and land the gig, but before you do that, you should first decide if this is the right opportunity for you. So when you find a potential speaking opportunity through an online search, referrals, SEO, or another one of the strategies we mentioned, ask yourself the following questions:

- *When is the event?* Has it already happened? Is there enough time before the next event? Usually you want to start reaching out to clients at least four to six months before the event. So if it's May and you come across an event that is happening in July, that event probably has already booked its speakers. Of course it's fine to take a shot if you want, but just know it's a long shot and your time may be better spent on something a little further out. But if it's happening in November, you should definitely reach out. They may tell you they're not booking speakers until July, but now you know when to follow up. It's always better to be too early than too late.
- *Do they bring in speakers?* Are there speakers on their website? Is anyone listed as a special guest or

keynote presenter? This is crucial. If they don't bring in speakers, don't try to convince them. Your time and energy are better spent on other opportunities.
- *What do these speakers talk about?* Whenever possible, look up information and agendas from previous years to see what topics were covered. This goes back to "interest." You want to make sure you speak about similar things as past speakers to ensure you're a good match for the event.
- *Who is the decision maker?* I'll show you exactly how to find out and what their titles usually are in chapter 14. But keep in mind when you're perusing these websites that you'll need to figure out whom to contact.

And that's how you find gigs. Now let's put it all together and start reaching out.

ACTION PLAN

1. Start by doing a simple online search to see what events are out there. Using every search term that applies to you, get as specific as you can, focusing on areas near where you live or that you'd be willing to travel to.

2. Run through the questions at the end of this chapter to see which events make the cut, and then make a list of potential gigs to reach out to.

3. Brainstorm a list of friends, previous clients, or other speakers you know who may be willing to refer business to you.

> BONUS: For more information on finding paid speaking gigs, including utilizing strategies like SEO and pay-per-click advertising, check out the free tools and resources at SpeakerBook Bonus.com.

14

Reaching Out to Potential Clients

I still remember that first email I sent to get that very first paid speaking gig for the Missouri 4-H event. My heart beat a little quicker, I perspired a bit (okay, a lot—and let me tell you: my body already loves to sweat), then hit Send. It wasn't particularly difficult once I had done the work of finding the client and reaching out, but it still took some courage. Secretly, I wondered if it was just a fluke that would never happen again, a one-time thing. So I tried again.

The next paid gig of my career was for an Indiana 4-H conference, and this time I quoted them $1,750 instead of $1,000, which felt like an astronomical amount of money to me then. The event planner didn't even balk at it, replying to my email and saying they could do that, no problem. After that, I realized how simple this is: you figure out who you want to speak to, what you want to say, how you're going to talk to them, and just start reaching out. This part of the job is really about putting in the hours. More than anything, it's a numbers game. For every offer you get, you'll get at least nine rejections.

So far, you've done most of the hard work—identifying an industry, developing your talk, and researching what kinds of events you should be targeting. Now that you know all that, you just need to reach out.

But how do you do that?

Finding the Right Person

First, you have to figure out whom to contact. Identifying decision makers is all about figuring out who makes the hiring decisions for an event, and this will be different for every event. Sometimes it will be the head of HR; other times it may be an outside event planner. It could even be the CEO or the company's founder. You just never know, so do your research and find out who you should be talking to.

Granted, it would be a lot easier if there were a title, such as "speaker booker," but that's not usually how it works. In all likelihood, you'll have to do a little bit of sleuthing, which will require you to scour their website, looking for the right person to contact.

In general, the smaller the event, the more likely the decision maker will be someone at the senior level, such as an executive director or manager. Other titles to look for include event coordinator, marketing director, and program director. For schools, it's often the principal or assistant principal who books the assemblies. Most likely, it won't be an assistant or intern. If it's not the person at the very top, they can refer you to the one who does make those decisions.

If you're unsure who the decision maker is, just ask. This may feel a little awkward at first, but it's completely normal. All you have to do is email the person who is your best guess for being the one in charge of booking speakers and say something like, "Do you mind my asking who is in charge of hiring speakers?" I've done this many times over the years, and it has worked quite well. Just know that a lot of these cold emails will be ignored, and that's okay. If you reach out to enough people, some will respond.

Once you find out who you should be speaking to, you can usually find their email address or phone number on the company's website. You may even be able to guess it; in my experience, this usually isn't that difficult as you experiment combining variations of their first and last name—such as first initial plus last name, first name plus last initial, full first name plus full last name, last name plus first name, and so on—at their company's website domain. For example, if you were trying to find my email, you could try the following: grantb@grantbaldwin.com; gbaldwin@grantbaldwin.com; grantbaldwin@grantbaldwin.com; and baldwingrant@grantbaldwin.com. You get the idea.

Email is going to be an easier way to contact people than via phone these days, but use whatever information you can find.

Before Contacting Decision Makers

Before we get to pressing Send on that email or picking up the phone to call the decision maker, let me give you some general tips for reaching out to people you don't know and who don't know you.

At first, do not try to sell them anything. A big mistake new speakers make is "going for the kill" right out of the gate, saying something like, "Hey, I just came across your site, and I'd love for you to book me." Think about that for a moment; it's like proposing on your very first date. The event planner has no idea who you are, no clue if you're any good, and every reason not to speak to you again. Remember that this is a relationship business. Your goal is to build connections with people, not just get gigs. If getting gigs is your only goal, event planners will be able to tell pretty quickly, and it may turn them off.

Understand that your only goal is to get a reply—that's it—not to get booked but to get them to respond. From there, you can build a connection and have a conversation to explore if you would be a good fit for each other. Try to think of this in terms of getting the person to take the next logical step. Maybe it's to get them to reply to your email, visit your website, or watch your video. It doesn't matter; just know what it is going into it and try to make it as easy as possible. You always want them to go one more step forward with you, never rushing them three steps ahead.

Before you make an ask, be sure to add value. This could be done any number of ways, but think about how you can help them somehow. It can be something as simple as saying, "I know you're in the customer service industry, and I came across this article that may be helpful for you." Or perhaps you can find an ebook, video, website, or resource you know would be a benefit to them that shows you're in touch with their needs.

Make sure that you already have your website in place before you reach out, so that you have something to show them. People will start investigating you without your having to say much. There have been times when I sent a simple, courteous email with a question, and someone responded with a speaking invitation. They tell me they went to my website and liked my stuff and ask if I'm available on a specific date. Don't get me wrong, it's not normally that easy, but sometimes it is. And you want to create every opportunity for yourself. When you crack that door open with your initial email, have everything in place so you can make room for a little luck.

Before reaching out, consider the best days and times to contact the client when you are most likely to get a reply. This is going to be different in every industry. Around the holidays is almost always a bad time to talk about this stuff, because most people are checked out and not making big decisions. For some industries, there are busier and slower times. For example, it's not a great time to email a school over the summer since most of their staff is in and out. You know your own industry, so think through those things before you just start contacting people on the weekend or in the middle of their vacation season.

How to Reach Out

Once you've done all that, here's how to contact decision makers:

- *Keep your email short and sweet.* One big mistake a lot of new speakers make is to send a ninety-four-paragraph email about why they are awesome and should be hired. Don't do that. Put yourself in the position of the client. These people are busy and don't have time to read long emails, let alone emails asking them for something. Keep it brief, and your chances of receiving a reply will dramatically increase.

- *Personalize the email.* Do not mass email a bunch of people with the same email or try to contact multiple event planners at the same time. Some people try to save time by collecting a thousand email addresses and sending out a generic pitch to them all, which doesn't work. Personalizing the email shows them that you did your research and that you care. It also shows you're not lazy and that you take this work seriously, which will impress them. Make sure when you send these emails that you do so from a personally branded email address, such as yourname@yourdomain.com. In the footer of your email, include a link to your website and some minimal information about who you are. All of this is branding and will create a sense of personalization and professionalism from the outset.
- *Ask a question.* Again, we're trying to get them to respond, and if it's short and easy, people feel compelled to answer one or two questions to initiate a dialogue. For example, you could ask, "When is your next event?" or "Who are some speakers you've worked with before?" or "Have you started planning your next conference?" Ask a specific question that doesn't require a long answer from them. Don't leave

the end of your email vague with no clear call to action or next step. Whatever question you ask, make sure the information is not readily available on their website. If you ask when their next event is and it's plastered all over their site, that doesn't look good.

- *Don't be a creepy stalker.* Don't send them an email and then a day or two later send another saying, "Hey, I haven't heard from you. Just following up." That gets annoying. You definitely should follow up, but give them some time. Recently, someone sent me an email, and I didn't immediately respond, so he continued to send me an email every day for the next week. Do you think that made me want to respond? No. It made me want to never hear from him again. Don't be that guy.
- *Wait two weeks before following up.* You may even want to develop some sort of system to schedule this for you so you don't have to worry about it. There are several software options that do this for you automatically. When following up, forward your previous email and say, "Hi, I sent you the below email a few weeks ago. Didn't hear back, so I wasn't sure if you got it. I know you're very busy, but if you get a second I'd love to hear from you." Forwarding your previous email gives them some context for who you are. If you send a brand-new email saying you haven't heard back, they're going to wonder who you are and might not even look through their email to find the original.
- *Follow up twice.* Then if they still don't reply, send a "ball in your court" email, which basically says,

"Hey, I've emailed you a few times and haven't heard anything back. I wasn't sure if you got my emails. I know you're busy and I don't want to be a bother. I'll leave the ball in your court. If you'd like to talk more, just let me know." Plenty of people won't reply to this, but those who were initially interested and got busy will say, "Oh sorry, I just forgot about this, but we're definitely interested." Many people feel bad because they didn't respond and that's enough to get them to respond.

The Phone Call

So far, we've only covered emailing people, but when should you pick up the phone? Whenever it's going to require a lot of back-and-forth to get the needed information.

For example, let's say they reply to your email and are interested in booking you but ask a question like, "Are you available on this date?" or "What are your fees?" or "What do you speak about?" If that happens, call them. Doing that shows them you're serious and that you can provide a high level of customer service. I've been booked before just from doing this, because it impressed the client. Imagine pressing Send on an email and five minutes later getting a phone call from the company saying they got your email and wanted to personally get back to you. This can make a big difference.

Calling can, of course, be intimidating, but you can usually sell yourself much better over the phone than via email. If it's a smaller gig or a free workshop, it's not as important to call, but if it's a keynote or a paid opportunity, you definitely need to call once they've responded to your initial proposal. But what, exactly, do you say, and how do you not botch the call?

Let's assume at this point you've got someone who sounds interested in booking you. Go, you! Well done. Now let's talk about how that initial phone call should go and what it takes to seal the deal without being "salesy."

To reiterate, how quickly you make that first phone call can make or break the deal. I don't say this to stress you out; I don't want you tied to your desk all day just waiting for a reply to your email, but it's important to make the call as soon as possible. If they reach out and don't hear from you for a week, they're going to assume you're not that serious or too busy. That's not the kind of speaker most clients want to work with. If you're great onstage but a pain to work with, you won't get booked, and you certainly won't build a successful speaking business that way. People want a great speaker, no doubt, but they also want someone who delivers on their promises and offers great customer service. This really is a customer service business: the client is the customer, and you are the business.

So here's how to sell without really selling:

Before you make that first call, do your homework. Look up when their event is, speakers they've had in the past, and any information on the person you're calling. What's their title and role at the company? What is the mission of the company? Learn anything you can so you're familiar with them.

When they answer, make sure they are free to talk. Say, "Did I catch you at a good time? Do you have a few minutes to chat?" This is a respect thing. Get their permission and don't assume they have all the time in the world. Go into the call with a clear idea of when they need to go, so you don't go over.

Next, build rapport. Try asking, "How is the year going for you?" Or even, "How long have you been in this role?" Try to ask questions you can't research ahead of time, so that you make the most of your time together and don't come across as unprepared. Remember, they're just a person, and you're just a person. Treat them like you'd want to be treated.

The next step is to learn about the event. A good transition is, "So tell me about your event." It's a casual invitation for them to talk, and your only job is to listen and ask questions. There's no need to sell yourself. Don't jump in and say you'd be perfect for this. Just ask follow-up questions like, "How many years have you had the conference? What speakers have you had in the past? What are some challenges that you've run into with other speakers? Who is your ideal audience member?" You're learning about the event.

Take notes during this time so you can repeat back what they said and be clear on what they need. They may say, "Well, last year's speaker was so hard to work with," or "The audience said they couldn't see the slides last time because of technical issues." This is all gold. They're telling you what they want you to tell them.

When responding, use all this information they just shared in your reply. You could say, "One of the things I do is make sure to provide a great customer service experience for you." Or "I don't often use slides in case of technical issues." Repeating back their concerns in this way lets them know you heard them and you're going to make sure that doesn't happen. It's reassuring. You'll also want to include this information in follow-up emails you send. Again, make sure you have a good note-taking system.

There are three main questions that they will most likely have for you:

- What do you speak about?
- Are you available on that date?
- What are your fees?

When they ask what you speak about, what you *don't* want to do is say, "Well, what do you want me to talk about?" or "I can talk about anything." Like we said in step 1, people want options. You want to walk through your programs and presentations, connecting them to what they just told you they need. For example, let's say the client says, "Our customer service team is having a big challenge with follow-up times and getting back to clients at a reasonable pace." You can be thinking, "I have three different presentations, and this particular one is going to be best for that and this is how I can tweak it a bit to address customer service to make sense for this audience." Just as a restaurant does, you can offer them something from your speaking menu, with minor adjustments to fit their unique tastes. Get as much information from them as possible so that when you walk through your presentations, you can connect it back to their needs.

Asking if you're available on a particular date is self-explanatory. I recommend using an online calendar with four different categories and four different colors. The first is called an "internal hold," which represents when you've spoken to a client and they have expressed interest in hiring you but haven't asked to hold the date yet. Go ahead and pencil that in with a particular color. Then there's the "client-requested hold," which is when a client has specifically asked you to hold a date, so it's fairly certain you will speak there. Use another color for that one. The third category is "contract pending," which means you have basically already booked the gig and sent them a contract, but you're just waiting to get it back. The fourth category is "confirmed event," which means you've received the contract and deposit, and it's a done deal.

When people ask about fees, respond by saying you have different options depending on what they're looking for. You will have a fee structure that we'll get into later. Then transition by asking something like, "Do you mind my asking what kind of budget you're trying to stay within?" Not only does this put the ball in their court, but it gives you some information before you start talking numbers. After they tell you, you can start walking them through your fee structure and packages.

After you quote your fee comes the hardest part: shutting up. I promise you this is a huge mistake new speakers make all the time, because talking about money can be awkward. A lot of people hem and haw and talk themselves down from their full fee, negotiating with themselves before the client even says a word. They may say, "My fee is usually $3,000, but it can be whatever you want." No, no, no—don't do that. It's okay to negotiate, especially when you're new, but say your fee with confidence and don't try to fill the silence until you hear back.

After the Call

So after you have that initial conversation, what happens next? The person you spoke to typically has to meet with a board, or a committee, or maybe just their boss to discuss possibly hiring you as a speaker for their event. Don't expect a decision right away. Even if you're speaking to the ultimate decision maker, they usually want to weigh their options and possibly get input from others. It's a longer sales process, so set your expectations accordingly.

Your next step is to figure out what their next step is, which is crucial. If they don't volunteer the information, ask them, and they'll probably tell you. It's perfectly acceptable to say, "So what's your next step in the process?" or "Do you know when you will be making a decision?" You want to get a time frame for your own follow-up purposes, so you can check back in without being annoying. Once you have some kind of time frame, ask permission to follow up. If they say, "We'll meet with our board in two months," you can say, "Great! Do you mind if I follow up with you then?" Almost all of them will tell you "absolutely." Clients rarely mind that, because they don't expect you to be so proactive, which is yet another way you can stand out.

So, of course, now you have to remember to follow up within whatever time frame they specified. If you say you'll follow up in two months, follow up in two months! This is a huge competitive advantage, because it's an area where most speakers drop the ball. I've picked up so many bookings over the years not because I'm the best speaker but because I followed up. The client said they were going to meet in two months, and I followed up, staying at the forefront of their mind, and was hired. If you end the call and say, "Okay, if you need anything else just let me know," don't hold your breath for the phone to ring. The secret is in the follow-up.

There are a lot of ways to do this: set a reminder on your phone, schedule an appointment on your calendar, use a customer relationship management (CRM) software, etc. You can even create your own system, but whatever you do, just don't forget. Even if they're interested, they may forget to get back to you when they said they would. To you, this gig may represent a huge breakthrough; to them, booking you is likely one among hundreds of details they need to take care of this month, so don't take it personally.

In addition to following up within the time frame they gave you, send an email within a day or two of the call with four items. The first is your presentation list, your speaking menu. You will have most likely gone over this on your call, but send it to them as a reminder. Second is the fee structure you went over. Third is any relevant testimonials. If the gig is a sales conference and you've already spoken at sales conferences, include testimonials from those events and clients. And lastly, a thank-you. Thank them for their time and for considering you. Send this all in one email with the necessary PDFs attached. If you want to go one step further, send a handwritten thank-you note.

ACTION PLAN

1. Start emailing! Email one decision maker this week. Bonus points if you can get a call scheduled.

2. Remember to follow up if you haven't heard from them in two weeks.

> BONUS: For more help with reaching out to potential clients, including a list of current tools to help you automatically schedule follow-up calls, samples of handwritten thank-you notes, and other resources, visit SpeakerBookBonus.com.

15

Closing the Deal

So you've been emailing and calling back and forth with a client and they've finally decided to book you. This is an amazing feeling; take a moment to enjoy it. You should be proud of yourself. But now what? Now it's time to close the deal. Let's go over what you should send them to get the ball rolling.

First, you'll want to send an email with the following documents attached:

- *Your speaker agreement.* This is your contract, but you don't necessarily have to use that term, as it can sometimes sound intimidating. Whatever you call it, keep it short. The more legalese you use, the more intimidating it is for the client to sign. If you're commanding six figures for a speech, maybe you want a contract with a lot of legal terms, but for most of us, we just need a document that lays out what we're

CLOSING THE DEAL

going to do and what they're going to do. Include all the client information: date, speaking details, topic of the talk, length of the talk, financial details, and travel information. You should also include that you require a 50 percent deposit up front, which is standard.

- *Event information form.* This is a sheet that the client fills out that will tell you everything about the event and local logistics. It should include not only where and when the event is but also details such as what airport you fly in to, what hotel you're staying in, what time you need to get there, when you can leave, who your onsite contact person is, etc. If the client is booking any travel for you, this form needs to include all relevant confirmation numbers and such.

- W-9. This is only if you are based in the U.S. The client will most likely send you a 1099 form at the end of the year for taxes. In order to do that, they'll need a W-9 from you.

- *Your speaking rider.* This document includes all of your preferences. If you're very early on in your career, you don't need to worry about this because you probably don't even know your preferences yet. But if you do, you can include things like your favorite mic, lighting setup, stage setup, and so on. Having this document will eliminate some back-and-forth between you and the client.

- *Promotional materials.* They will probably ask for this to add to their website and help promote the event, so it's helpful to just send it over right away. This includes things like your headshot and bio. Ideally, you should have these uploaded to a website like Dropbox or Google Drive where they can download the high-resolution version of these files without you having to attach them to an email.

Next, it's time to ask for a deposit. As I mentioned above, 50 percent is practically universal in the speaking industry. On some occasions, this may be a problem for the client if, for example, they're funded by a grant and aren't receiving any money to pay you up front. Some government organizations aren't allowed to pay deposits either. Make your own decision if this is the case, but I always let it go and trust the client to pay in full closer to or after the date. If their hands are tied, there's nothing you can do. Just make sure you get the speaker agreement back and amend it with these details.

When you receive all these documents, you'll need to sign the agreement, scan it, and send it back to them so they have a copy as well. Keep these documents in a safe, organized place where you can easily access them, such as a folder in a secure, cloud-based application that you can access from anywhere.

What to Charge

When it comes to speaking, the client is paying for three specific things. First, they're paying for your knowledge, which is worth so much more than the hour you spend onstage and includes the years it took to acquire that knowledge. Second, they're paying for the delivery of that knowledge, because, after all, it doesn't matter how much you know if you're terrible at communicating it. They're not only paying for your presentation but the time and attention it took to practice it so that you could deliver it effortlessly for a live audience. And lastly, they're paying for your time, or as I like to joke with clients: they're not paying me to come speak, they're paying me to leave my family. Think of your speaking fee as the culmination of all these three factors coming together, not just the few hours you're actually at the event. Although speaking fees vary widely, depending on the industry, a basic breakdown follows:

$1,000–$5,000
Education industry
New speakers

$5,000–$10,000
Up-and-coming corporate speakers with some experience

$10,000–$20,000
Professional speakers with a lot of experience

$20,000–$50,000
Bestselling authors
Professional athletes
B-list celebrities

$50,000+
Celebrities

It may seem crazy to talk about making this much money standing on a stage talking for an hour, but as long as you're providing more value than you cost, you're worth whatever you charge. That's why celebrities can charge so much money: they tend to draw a huge crowd, which turns into more tickets sold for the event. If you can help a company bring in an additional $50,000 of revenue and you only cost $10,000, that's a deal. Even if it's more difficult in your industry to put a monetary amount on the value you add, this is an important mind-set shift to make: from "it's crazy anyone would pay me that" to "I'm providing real value for other people." Because you are.

Where do you start, though? If you're just getting started as a speaker, I recommend setting your initial fee at $1,000, which may sound crazy if you've never been paid to speak before, but this is a realistic number in most industries and the going rate for new speakers. That said, be willing to negotiate, especially at the beginning, varying your rate based on the client's budget. In some cases, they may have less than $1,000, which is totally normal. In response, you could say, "My typical fee is $1,000, but I'm willing to do it for $500." Sometimes, you have to do it for even less than that if that's all the client has. When you're starting out, you need the experience, so take what you can get, including the occasional free or low-paying gig. The goal is to practice, build relationships, and get some testimonials.

At some point, though, you will need to start believing in your value enough to charge a fee. For my very first fee, I was charging $1,500 for up to three talks (typically a keynote and two breakout sessions), plus travel. That worked out to about $500 per talk, but it was just as much work for me to do three presentations as it was to do one. I figured that as long as I was there, I might as well give as many presentations as possible.

Determining Your Fee

Here's how to get started with pricing:

- *Create a fee structure with options.* This should accompany your speaking menu that you email to the client. A fee structure allows you to not have to pull a number out of thin air when people ask you what you charge, and it gives you confidence. Clients will also be less likely to try to negotiate with you if it's right there on the page that you emailed them after your call.
- *Make your fee structure easy to understand.* Include all the details a client may need about what they're paying for. Also remember, if you're in more than one industry, you may need to have different fee structures for each industry. This probably won't apply when you're getting started, since you should aim for one industry at a time. Years ago when I was transitioning from speaking to high schools and colleges to speaking to corporations, I had to have three different fee structures because the audiences and budgets were so different and the clients needed different options.
- *Don't post your fees on your website.* The client should contact and connect with you before they

discover your fee. If you put it on your website, they will see it and say, "Well, we don't have the budget, so this speaker's not a possibility," when in reality you may be willing to negotiate or there may be some other way to work it out. Some higher-level speakers who charge five figures post their fees as a filter to weed out people who can't afford them, but unless that's you, I suggest not putting your numbers on your website.

- *Always give the client more than what they paid for.* I have heard event planners say about other speakers, "They were good, but they weren't $5,000 good. I think we overpaid." You never want someone to say that about you. In fact, you want them saying the opposite: "I can't believe we got that talk for that price! I feel like we got a deal." People want to feel like they got a bargain, not like they were ripped off, so if you're going to err, err on the low side—not because you don't know your worth or because you're not confident, but because you want to over-deliver on what was expected. Plus, it's much easier to raise your fees than lower them.
- *Raise your fees cautiously.* Don't make huge leaps. Think of it like the occupancy rate for a hotel: If the hotel is constantly booked because people love it, then it's time to raise the rates. But if your "hotel" isn't fully booked yet and you're still having trouble getting customers at that price, you probably want to stick to that price for a while longer, until demand grows. If you are consistently getting booked at your

current fee with little to no pushback, it's probably time to raise your rates.

Who pays for travel? There are typically two ways this works; I've done both ways. The first is you book your own travel and invoice it separately from the event. That means they pay you your fee, then you keep track of your travel receipts and after the event get reimbursed by the client. The upside to this is that you get completely covered for all your travel expenses. The downside is that sometimes the cost may surprise the client, and no one likes that. Maybe they didn't expect your flight or rental car to cost so much. If they were budgeting $750 and you spent $1,200, they're not going to like that, and it leaves a bad taste in their mouth, even if you did everything you could to keep the costs down. You may feel like you have to justify why you spent that amount on something. Sometimes it can also take time to get reimbursed, and it's more for you to keep track of, which can honestly turn into a bit of a headache.

The second way to do travel expenses is to simply include it in your fee as one lump sum. The upside to this approach is it's much easier for you to keep track of and for the client to budget. There are no surprises, and in some cases, you may actually make money on it. You also get paid more quickly, because the client will have paid it ahead of time. The downside is you could potentially lose money with travel expenses ending up being more than you expected.

An alternative is to charge a flat travel fee, so instead of saying your rate is $6,000, travel included, you could say it is $5,000 plus a $1,000 travel fee. There's not a big difference, really, other than showing exactly how much you allot yourself for travel. Quick tip: If you're speaking at a conference, you can ask if they'll cover your room; often they have discounted or comped rooms for conferences, and that can help cut down on costs as well. You never know until you ask.

Should You Speak for Free?

Speaking of fees, should you ever speak for free? Speaking for free is a little controversial in our business, as people tend to have strong opinions on the subject. We're going to dig into the pros and cons of it, though, because I think it's a misconception to assume speaking for free is always bad. Of course, you can't make a living speaking for free, but it can be a smart strategy to get more gigs, if you leverage it the right way.

Some of this goes back to your speaking goals. If speaking is just a hobby, then you may not be interested in making a lot of money from it, in which case speaking for free may be just fine with you. But even then, I believe that if you are providing real value for people, then you should be compensated for that value. There is nothing wrong with being paid to do something, even if you are just doing it because you think it's fun or because you're trying to help people. I recommend you learn to get comfortable with that if you are not already. But sometimes it can be smart to speak for free, as long as you know why you're doing it, which is the most important part.

Some speakers speak for free without any real reason why. As a result, it doesn't have the intended effect, and they may even end up feeling taken advantage of. How is this benefiting your brand? How is it benefiting your personal life? Will it get you more speaking gigs? First, you must establish your value before talking numbers. Remember when I said one of the first things they're going to ask you is, "What is your fee?" This is why we want to get them on the phone: because if you just present a number, the lowest bid will probably win—and you don't want to be in a position where it's a race to the bottom. This is why you want to go through all your different presentations and explain what you offer, how you can customize it, and what they're getting. All this information should be in their mind before you mention numbers, so they understand the value.

Negotiating can be scary, but it doesn't have to be hard. Sometimes we think we have to have an us-versus-them mentality, but the best negotiating is done when you're trying to create a win-win situation for both of you. Both parties need to feel like they've given and received tremendous value. The hardest thing for a speaker to do is walk away from an opportunity. Obviously, your goal is to speak, but sometimes you start going back and forth with a client, and for one reason or another, it doesn't work out. If you get the feeling that this is going to be a losing situation for either of you, walk away. You're offering significant value as a speaker and can't give it away for free all the time. There are some situations when it's worth it to discount your fee, but there are some when it just won't make sense. You have to be comfortable saying no.

That said, sometimes there's just not a lot of money in the budget or due to special circumstances, you shouldn't walk away. You may want to take the occasional free or low-paying gig. But how do you know when? Below are some scenarios when it actually does make sense.

ACQUIRE PAID SPEAKING GIGS

1. *For multiple bookings.* An organization hired me for two events then later reached out to do a third and then a fourth. Eventually, they asked, "What if we hired you for ten events this year; could we get some kind of package deal?" Of course. That's a huge win for me, and I'd much rather work with one client on ten engagements than try to find nine more on my own, so we did a significant discount on each gig since they were booking so many.
2. *Spin-off business.* This is when you speak somewhere and get additional bookings from that engagement. If you have an opportunity to speak at an event where you're likely to get more business, it may make sense to take a lower fee or maybe even do it for free to get the extra business.
3. *Less travel is involved.* I'm almost always willing to negotiate or take a lower fee if it means I won't be away from home long. At our house we always say, "How many sleeps is Daddy gone?" Anytime I can speak somewhere nearby with zero missed "sleeps," that's a huge win for me.
4. *It's a fun place to visit.* I'm often willing to negotiate on places where I can bring my family. I've always said, only half jokingly, that I'm willing to speak for free in Hawaii if you pay for my family to come. We haven't made it to Hawaii yet, but my wife and I did recently stay for free at a resort in the Philippines for five days thanks to a speaking gig.
5. *It's a slower time of year.* You'll find some seasons are busier than others, and for most speakers, spring

and fall are when most conferences and events happen. So summer and winter are pretty slow. Going back to our hotel analogy, if it's a slow season and you're trying to entice clients, you may lower your costs or create some incentive.

6. *Potential product sales.* I've had a few events where I actually made more money in product sales than from my speaking fee. If you have a product and sell it at events, you'll begin to get a feel for events where it sells really well. Sometimes, you may just want to get in front of an audience to sell your product and not even worry about a speaking fee.

7. *Lead generation for a back-end product or service.* You may have a book, training program, or coaching program, and this event could be a lead-generation tool for that resource. You're not actually selling it at the event, but speaking allows you to capture leads that you can later convert into sales.

8. *Video footage.* You can negotiate a lower speaking fee with a client in exchange for demo video footage. At many conferences a film crew is on-site, and if you want some of that footage, this may be worth speaking for free.

9. *To get more practice.* This will be the primary reason you speak for free as a beginner. The only way to get better is to practice, and sometimes that means taking what you can get, even if it's nothing. If possible, try to do this locally so you're not out a bunch of money for travel and hotel.

10. *Credibility.* TEDx Talks are not paid, but there's certainly a big benefit to doing one. There may be other

events in your industry similar to that where being onstage would be a huge boost to your credibility and thus worth speaking for free.
11. *You want to attend the conference anyway.* Sometimes I offer to do a free session in exchange for complimentary admission to a conference I wanted to attend anyway. This way, I at least get a free ticket and some extra speaking practice.
12. *To build a relationship with the client.* If there is a client or company you want to continue to work with, speaking for free at first is a great way to get your foot in the door and to build a relationship. Don't explicitly say, "I'm doing this one for free but I expect to get paid in the future," but do share what your normal speaking fee for that gig would be, and communicate that you hope to do more business with them in the future.

One way to negotiate with clients who have smaller budgets is to suggest splitting the cost with another group. A few years ago I was speaking at a major university. The department hiring me couldn't afford my lowest package, but another department within the university was having an event as well, so the two departments split the cost of a package for two talks and I delivered one to each. Let's say you're going to speak at a corporation; maybe the HR department could pay for one talk and the sales department could pay for another.

Another option for negotiation is to offer additional value. You could say, "My speaking fee is X, but we can include additional presentations or books or coaching or consulting, etc." This doesn't require lowering your fee, but it may still save them money. Some conferences have different areas within the budget for resources or training. If you include books or a workshop, they may be able to split your fee from their end in such a way that it saves them money in the training or resources department.

ACTION PLAN

1. Determine your speaking fee and create a fee structure. Decide under what circumstances you would speak for free.

2. Once a client has decided to book you, send them an email with your speaking agreement, event information form, W-9, speaking rider, and promotional materials.

3. Ask for the deposit, usually 50 percent.

> BONUS: For an example of a one-page fee structure sheet, visit SpeakerBookBonus.com.

16

Customer Service and Repeat Business

The best way to stay in this business for a long time is to learn how to relate well to people. If you can deliver a great talk, provide a high-quality experience, and stay in touch with people, you will have a long speaking career.

I've already shared with you the importance of follow-up; it is the lifeblood of this kind of business—you can't survive without it. Now that we've learned how to get the speaking gigs you want and why you should sometimes strategically work for free, let's look at how to leverage those relationships into a lifetime of speaking opportunities.

Your Best Marketing Is You

First of all, as I've mentioned throughout this entire book, the best marketing you'll ever do is to be great at what you

CUSTOMER SERVICE AND REPEAT BUSINESS

do. One of the best ways to get more business as a speaker is from someone who sees you speak live, whether they end up referring you to a friend or booking you themselves. Again, you have to get out there and take what you can get, because speaking tends to lead to more speaking.

Some clients won't ever book you if they haven't first seen you live, so if you already have a speaking gig, see if you can invite a potential client in the area to come. This accomplishes two goals: first, they get to see you live, and second, it shows them that you are already in demand, since you're inviting them to a gig. Event planners want to book speakers who are already speaking.

Research other potential clients in the area who may be interested in seeing you speak. Maybe there are more event planners in the area who would hire you as well. Look them up and invite them to an event, shooting them an email that says, "Hi, I wanted to let you know I'm going to be speaking at X event on this date and time. I'd love to meet you." Of course, you'd want to ask your client's permission to invite someone from outside the organization if it's a private event.

I once invited a potential client to see me speak at a high school assembly in Oregon. The potential client and I had never met and she'd never seen me speak before she accepted my invitation. After the event, she booked me right on the spot. Live presentations are extremely effective for booking more gigs, which is why we spent so much time on preparing your talk. As I've mentioned, the best marketing you can do is to have a great talk.

For this reason, national conferences are excellent gigs, because many decision makers in that industry will be there to see you. Even if that isn't your favorite kind of gig, it can be a good opportunity, since a lot of people in that room will be from different states or countries and have their own organizations that need speakers. Early on, I did a lot of conferences, because I knew the five hundred or so students in that room represented at least fifty different schools, which was a lot of potential events in need of a speaker.

Another early gig was at a Future Business Leaders of America conference in Oklahoma for an audience of no more than two hundred people. They paid me $500, and I had to cover my own travel, which means it was basically a break-even event for me. However, the wife of the national director of the association happened to be there, and right after the event, she called her husband and told him to hire me. The next year I did the opening keynote at all three of their national conferences and earned a lot more than $500. That little state conference taught me that even when you are speaking, maybe even especially then, you are also marketing.

Creating a Great Client Experience

Be good to people. That's rule numero uno. After you get the gig, your goal is to be the kindest, easiest speaker this person has ever worked with. This really is a customer service business after all, and how well you take care of your clients will determine how long (or short) your career is.

You want to make sure that the process is as smooth and simple as it can possibly be for the client. Don't make complicated requests or have ridiculous needs. If you need something, most likely you can take care of it yourself. The only thing I ever ask for from a client is a couple bottles of water.

The speaker is one small part of an event. I know it feels like a big deal to you, but there are so many moving pieces, and event planners have a lot on their mind. The more low-maintenance you can be, the better. Try to be even better offstage than you are on. Clients love it when you interact with the audience offstage, attend some other sessions, or attend one of the meals. Don't be the speaker who bounces in and bounces out. Try to mingle and answer questions. It shows you're continuing to add value to the event, even when you're not onstage.

If you don't want to constantly be meeting new prospects and introducing yourself to hundreds of potential clients each year, then I suggest you learn how to deliver a stellar experience for your clients so they want to keep bringing you back. The best way to get rebooked for an event is for the client and event staff to have a great experience with you. When organizations have hired me for multiple events, it was because I made their job easier. Yes, your job is to speak, but it's also to provide a top-notch experience for the client.

Here's how you can do just that.

Before the Event

First, connect with the audience before the event starts. One way to do this is, if possible, to request an email database of all the attendees and send them a short email introducing yourself. When you ask the client for the email addresses, make it clear you plan to send the attendees one email before the event and one email after, and that's it. The client will feel protective of their attendees' contact information, and that's normal. They want to make sure you're not going to spam them or sell the list to someone else.

In the email before the event say something like, "Hey, my name is Grant. I'm going to be the keynote speaker at X conference. I'm really looking forward to it. Please be sure to stop by and say hey. I'd love to meet you. Can't wait to see you there." Just something simple like that. Often the client sees this as a win because most speakers don't do that, and it's a good opportunity to differentiate yourself and the event.

Sometimes the client will offer to send out an email on your behalf, which is fine too. If this is not possible, you can always find a way to connect with attendees via social media or out front at the actual event before you go onstage. The point is to demonstrate that you are there to do more than simply speak for forty-five minutes.

Two weeks before the event, do a pre-event call to the client. Confirm all the final details like travel, schedule, speaking details, topic, etc. When you get booked three to six months out, there's a good chance something is going to change between then and the event. You probably haven't had contact with the client for months, which is why it's a good idea to circle back and confirm everything. That's also why you want to have a system for filing all your documents, so you can easily access your info sheet and make sure you have all the details for the event straight.

One week before the event, send an email confirming all the arrangements. At this point, you should have received a 50 percent deposit up front via check or however you preferred to be paid (the industry standard is check or direct deposit). The rest of your speaking fee is due at the time of the event. Remind the client of this, and discourage them from mailing you anything at this point, since this can sometimes take weeks depending on where they are located and how they ship it. Let them know you expect the rest of your fee at the event, not afterward.

During the Event

As I mentioned in chapter 8, you want to connect with as many people as possible at the event. This creates an impression for the client that you are there to serve them and their vision. Not only is this helpful for the performance side of things, it's also excellent customer service.

To help you make sure everything goes smoothly, you should make a one-sheet summary with all the details of the event boiled down on it, including travel schedule, speaking schedule, who the client is, where you're staying, talk topic, whether they owe you money, etc. This is just a simple administrative tool to help you stay on track and keep things running smoothly.

At the event, be sure to say your thank-yous. I recommend giving the client a handwritten thank-you card in person. I travel with a stack of these and write the note at the event after my speech. It's something simple I've been doing for years and has been a game changer for me in wowing clients and maintaining a great relationship long after the gig is over.

After the Event

After the event, I follow up with another thank-you note to the client that I put in the mail a few days later.

Sometimes I request their boss's information and send him or her a note as well, which makes the client look good. If the boss is at the event, I do it there; otherwise, I drop the note in the mail as soon as I get home. If CEO Bob has hired Joe the event planner, and you write to Bob to say what a fantastic time you had and how wonderful it was to work with Joe, Joe looks awesome! Now Joe loves you and is likely to hire you again. And Bob is likely to hire Joe again, so everybody wins. Sometimes, if it was a particularly great experience and a well-paying event, I send a physical gift like cookies or some other small token of my appreciation. I may even ask my assistant to put a thank-you note in the mail to all the logistics people she interacted with. You may not have time to write multiple thank-you notes, so do what you can, but I have never had someone tell me, "Grant, you thanked us too much." Very few speakers send these notes, but it's something that takes fifty cents and about thirty seconds to do and will help you stand out from the majority of people in your industry. Why not go the extra mile?

If possible, after the event send an email thanking everyone for attending and refer them to your website. This can be as simple as, "Hi, this is Grant. I was the opening keynote speaker at X conference. I had a wonderful time, and I met so many great people. If you're interested in more information, check out my site here." This follow-up lets people connect with you after the conference, and again, the goal is not to sell them anything but to simply connect and let them know who you are. It's all intended to create a positive impression with the client, assuring them that they made the right decision to hire you.

If your event fee wasn't inclusive, meaning travel wasn't included, now is when you will need to send your travel invoice. Create a system for this sort of thing so it is simple and automatic. Every time I book an event, it sets in motion a system that creates all the documents and email reminders of everything my team and I need to remember. In general, you want to become disciplined at keeping good records, as this will save you a lot of time and hassle later on. A mentor once told me when I was getting started that a paper trail is a safe trail. It's important to get everything you have agreed to in writing. If you don't have it in writing, then it didn't or won't happen.

Repeat Business (Make New Friends but Keep the Old)

Even if you're an excellent speaker, most clients will bring you back only after three or four years have passed. A lot of the same people attend yearly conferences, and event planners don't typically want audience members to hear the same speakers over and over again, which means for repeat business you need a system to follow up with these people.

If it fits with your industry, look for clients who have a new audience each year. For example, a few colleges and universities I work with have me come in every single year for new student orientation because it's a new audience every time. New staff trainings or orientations are settings where this also may apply, and if that's your ideal audience, it would be a good strategy to target these kinds of groups.

Many speakers who have been in the industry for over ten years tell me that 90 percent of their business is repeat.

They just work with the same rotation of clients every three to five years, so maintaining these relationships really matters, and it's something you'll want to systematize as early as possible. Be great at what you do, be good to people, and keep following up—do that and you'll never have to worry about running out of speaking gigs again.

ACTION PLAN

1. Decide on your speaking fee and structure.

2. Create your speaker agreement, rider, event information form, and promo materials.

3. Create a great client experience by setting up a pre-event call and creating a one-sheet summary of the event details.

REVIEW: STEP 4

1. Do a Google search and see how many search terms you can come up with and opportunities you can find to speak.

2. Find one speaking gig to pitch yourself for and identify the decision maker. Look for the titles we talked about or find some contact information of someone you can ask.

3. Identify at least one event planner with whom to start a dialogue and send that email.

4. Prepare your speaker agreement.

5. Decide what your fee should be. Create a fee structure with your presentation options and travel.

6. Decide under what circumstances you are willing to speak for free.

> BONUS: Use the fee structure template and the other free tools and resources at SpeakerBookBonus.com to help guide you in this step.

STEP 5
KNOW WHEN TO SCALE

If you're reading this book, you probably love speaking, which is great. I do too. But we all face the same limit: time. There is a limited amount of it, and as a speaker, you're only making money if you're onstage speaking. That time comes at a cost. The gig itself is great, but you have to pitch the gig, prepare the talk, make the slides, coordinate with the event planners, make the calls, send the emails, travel to the gig, and deliver the talk. This can get tiring for even the most dedicated of speakers, and burnout is a real possibility.

In this part we'll begin to explore how to build your business beyond the stage and what it means for you to grow your business as a speaker.

There are really only two ways to make more money, no matter what you do. You can either increase your prices or sell more. For the next few chapters, we'll talk about how to do that and how you can diversify your portfolio to complement your work as a speaker and ultimately increase your income.

17

Diversifying Your Income Streams

For twenty years, Kendra Dahlstrom worked in high-tech Silicon Valley, climbing the corporate ladder but never quite feeling fulfilled. She kept thinking that happiness would come when she reached the next level, but it never did, not even after she became an executive.

This feeling of angst only heightened when Kendra became a mother and finding purpose in her work became even more important. If she was going to spend most of the day away from her children, it had better be for a good reason. She negotiated with her employer to be able to work from home and moved out to a rural farming community in California, and she went to the office just once a month. She had it all: flexibility, freedom to be with her family, and financial security. And still, something was missing.

She recalled an experience in her twenties when she had been sexually harassed at work and wondered if perhaps her calling was to educate women on this important subject. Kendra reached out to a few experts on the subject and realized educating women on sexual harassment, as important a subject as it was, wasn't exactly what she was looking to do. However, in the process she discovered speaking.

After some reflection, Kendra felt that she needed to talk about leadership, since having been a leader at a Fortune 500 company was an important part of her story and expertise. "I realized I wanted to share a story about leadership that was the opposite of Joseph Campbell's monolith—heroes as assertive, aggressive personalities," she said. "People forget that leaders can be humble, selfless introverts who support and lift others up around them." Kendra wanted to work with females in corporate America whose soft skills were exactly what made them great leaders.

It was around this time that she joined my Booked and Paid to Speak course, and she landed her first major gig at the National Association of Realtors six months later. The event was hosted in Washington, DC, and they paid for her hotel, first-class airfare, and a $5,000 speaking fee. Within two months, Kendra had spoken at three major events, and within a year she had booked fifteen paid speaking engagements. After Kendra started speaking, people began to ask her to coach them. At first, she wasn't sure. "People kept coming to me asking for coaching," she recalled, "and I was like, well, I don't really know if I can coach. Then I realized the way in which I led people in organizations . . . I've always kind of coached."

Kendra fell in love with coaching. Not only was it in her wheelhouse, but it offered a more flexible and scalable business model than speaking. "You have the flexibility to create what you want," she said. "I went into it thinking I'd be 90 percent speaking, 10 percent coaching, but now I'm 90 percent coaching, 10 percent speaking, and it has totally worked for me. And if I wanted to flip that model again, I could do that."

Today, with two small children at home, Kendra takes only a handful of speaking engagements each year, with her fee typically ranging from $7,500 to $10,000 each. She specializes in helping people with six-figure businesses get to seven figures and beyond. She enjoys working with clients who have tried lots of business and marketing programs but still feel stuck. People in those situations tend to get in their own way and don't realize what's going on beneath the surface, which is where Kendra really shines.

At a certain point in your speaking career you may wonder, as Kendra did, if this is all there is. Certainly, some speakers just want to speak, and there's nothing wrong with that, but speaking can lead to all kinds of other opportunities that go beyond performing on a stage. Adding a new revenue stream to your speaking can be great for your business, but you just may end up like Kendra, with a completely different business model than the one you expected. And that's okay too. It's part of the process. In fact, that's exactly what happened to me.

When It's Time for a Change

In 2014 I had gotten to a place where I was doing seventy gigs a year. I was speaking on a lot of large, international stages and had someone helping me run the business side of things. But I found myself asking, what's next? Am I going to do this for the next twenty to thirty years? Plenty of people do. It's a great living, and there's nothing wrong with it, but I wanted something different—to keep mixing it up, trying new things, and finding new ways to grow my business.

That year while speaking at an event in Reno, Nevada, I got together with my friend Phil, who has been an inspiration and mentor to me. He's been in the speaking business for a long time, but what I admire most about Phil is what a great husband and father he is. We met up at a state park and walked around looking at the beautiful lakes and mountains and talking.

After lunch we walked out on a pier, and while we stood there looking out over the water, Phil said, "There are some people who just love speaking so much that's all they ever want to do. They'll do it forever and ever till the day they die. I'm an example of that. But Grant, you seem like an entrepreneur who just happens to be good at speaking. When you first start speaking, the challenge exceeds the skill set. You feel like you're way over your head and it's just overwhelming. But what happens is, over time, those start to reverse and eventually your skill set exceeds the challenge. You want to regularly find ways to put yourself in situations where you feel like you're a bit over your head in a good, healthy way." That really resonated with me. I felt like I was ready for a new challenge but didn't know what it was.

For the rest of this section, we're going to be talking about the business side of speaking and how you can maximize your income from speaking, including growing the business in the direction of not speaking. There are plenty of reasons to scale, and a few ways to tell if you're ready. One is to consider your stage of life. If you're single and full of energy, maybe speaking a hundred or more times a year is completely fine and in sync with your rhythm of life. But if you're married with kids, as I am, you may not want to do that anymore. It may be time for a change.

As I mentioned at the beginning of this book, your speaking business needs to be in alignment with the Topic Trifecta: industry, interest, and integrity. This is just as true for scaling your business. There needs to be a market for what you're offering (industry); you need to be knowledgeable and passionate about your topic (interest); and you need to be qualified to teach it to others (integrity). As we explore the various products you can add to your speaking business, and all the tactics for selling them, be sure to keep your own area of authority in mind. For your speaking business to grow cohesively, all of your efforts must be in alignment with who you are and where you're headed in life.

The Income Pie

Before you can create new products for your business, start scaling, or even begin diversifying your income streams, you need to get an accurate picture of where your money is coming from. Often, we speakers tend to work *in* our businesses, not *on* them, causing us to lose sight of which efforts are bearing the most fruit. You may have a general idea of where the money is coming from, but a detailed accounting of your income and expenses can help you get clarity on where you are at with your business and where you can grow.

To get a picture of your various income streams, begin by taking a look at the past year of revenue. If you can look back further, that's even better. As you do this, identify all the income sources you currently have, which should include speaking, of course, but may also include another part-time job, affiliate revenue, client work, selling crafts, pet sitting, or whatever else you may have. Quantify the total amount from each source as accurately as possible. Go back and look at your invoices or your taxes if necessary; just try to be as accurate as possible. Don't write down what you hoped it would be; write down what it actually was. I call this the "Income Pie."

Next, look at your total income for this time period and calculate what percentage each of these sources makes up. Let's say speaking is 30 percent of your revenue, and maybe your part-time job is 40 percent. Do some quick math to figure out which of your income sources is producing the most revenue for you. When you're finished, rank your sources of income. Are you surprised by some of the areas in which you are making money? Could you spend more time focusing on those areas to increase that amount? Are there areas in which you thought you were excelling that you are not?

After that, compare the income rankings and the percentages to the time you spend on these things. Do they match up? Do you spend the most time on your highest-income-producing activities? Or are there things that you're working hard on but seeing very little return from? These may be opportunities for you to cut back on certain business activities and free up more time to focus on more profitable ventures. Or maybe you'll discover the opposite, such as some successful sources of revenue that you haven't put much effort into at all that would be opportunities for you to ramp up your efforts in those areas to see even bigger gains.

As you do this, you will also want to evaluate these revenue streams, not just by amount, but also by how much you enjoy each of them. Are there things you don't enjoy or that you'd like to cut out? Can your budget take a hit on that amount of revenue if you decide to drop something? Or will you need to make it up somewhere else? Maybe the hit is worth it to you because of how much you dislike that activity, but you want to at least be aware of the amount of income you will lose if you decide to shift your business in a new direction.

The final step in this process, after you've examined your Income Pie, is to visualize the ideal state of your business. What changes do you want to make in your Income Pie chart to hit your ideal income? Think about the work balance you're looking for and the different ways you produce value for clients. Are you actually working on the things you enjoy, or are you just doing what you need to do to stay afloat? This boils down to three simple questions: What do you need to keep doing? What do you need to stop doing? And what do you need to start doing? And then ask: What steps do you need to take in order to make that happen? This can be a jarring experience, as you may find that your business isn't what you thought it was, in either positive or negative ways. But this is an important exercise because you're making decisions about where you want your money to come from in the future and what part speaking will play.

Seven Types of Speakers

When it comes to generating revenue, there are seven basic types of speakers, and they all have different Income Pies. Deciding which kind of speaker you want to be will be helpful in deciding what offerings you want to create and what your next steps are.

Type 1: The Super Speaker

These are people who get the vast majority of their income from speaking. In many cases super speakers travel a lot because being onstage is their primary path to income. These people usually have years of experience, both as a speaker and often in a previous career that gives them authority to speak on their given subject.

Super speakers are usually keynote speakers, because they command the highest fees, which allows them to do the fewest number of gigs for the most revenue. If you do twenty gigs at $20,000 each, that's $400,000 per year, which is a fantastic income. Some super speakers don't command that much per talk, but to make up for it, they speak a lot, maybe doing fifty or so gigs a year at $5,000 per gig. Sometimes they even have big enough names to host their own events and profit from ticket sales instead of only relying on speaker fees.

Erick Rheam, whom I mentioned at the beginning of this book, is a great example of a super speaker. He loves to travel and inspire new groups of people all the time. If you are going to be a super speaker, you had better love speaking and be willing to do it for a long time. Otherwise, another speaker type may work better for you.

Type 2: The Teacher

Teachers are speakers who earn a significant part of their revenue from speaking but balance that with income from

DIVERSIFYING YOUR INCOME STREAMS

online or in-person courses and programs, such as a membership site. These people package and sell their deep knowledge to their audience and other potential students. Teachers often lead workshops and create content where they can offer a sneak peek of the type of information that their courses offer. They can ask for higher prices for their workshops and breakout sessions given their experience with effecting change for attendees.

Dustin Hogan, whom we met in chapter 4, is an example of this speaker type, with his seminars and workshops. He does keynotes so that he can invite people to his smaller, higher-end events, which is a great way to funnel in new business as a teacher.

Type 3: The Influencer

These are people who make their money from a combination of speaking and monetizing their influence. Affiliate marketing, paid ads in large email newsletters or via social media, and paid posts on a big site are all examples of how influencers leverage their audiences. Speaking is often a path to broadening their audience and influence, which can lead to more money.

Influencers focus on capturing their audience as subscribers on an email list or followers on social media so they can market to these people later on. Because of this, they often have very active social accounts, a successful email newsletter, and/or a big blog or website. For this type, speaking is a means to an end, a way to generate leads to grow the audience, which can then be monetized later. Influencers don't necessarily worry about making a lot off their speaking as long as it provides them an opportunity to grow their influence, which is how they will grow their income.

Type 4: The Industry Expert

People trust industry experts on a very specific topic, and these people get paid to share their expertise in several forms. First, industry experts leverage their deep knowledge in a given area to make money through books and other information products. Second, industry experts make money from speaking. They are often highly sought-after keynote speakers in their industry, given their authority and name recognition. However, as an industry expert, you are often speaking at smaller industry events, including yearly conferences and other association gatherings. These speakers sometimes negotiate lower rates in exchange for book purchases or back-of-room sales, as this can be an important income stream for them. Dr. Sue Ettinger, the veterinarian who speaks on pet cancer (see chap. 1), is an example of an industry expert.

Type 5: The Coach

Coaches are speakers who make money from speaking as well as one-on-one or group coaching. They likely have training or deep expertise in a specific process, industry, or career and see their speaking as a means to attract new clients. These speakers are likely to do keynotes, but they also do workshops that facilitate change and prove their value as a coach. They may even run paid workshops and mastermind groups of their own. Kendra Dahlstrom, whom we met earlier in this chapter, is a great example of a coach.

Type 6: The Consultant

Consultants are speakers who also generate income by consulting for businesses or organizations that need their skills and advice. They may sometimes accept smaller fees when the audience they're speaking to will likely lead to more consulting clients. They do keynotes, but also workshops and seminars where they can demonstrate their deep knowledge and give the audience a taste of how they may be able to help those organizations and businesses through consulting. They may speak to an association audience in the hope of getting in front of their ideal audience to offer higher-end consulting services. Melanie Deziel, the woman who used her journalism experience to become a speaker (see chaps. 1 and 2), is a great example of a consultant who goes a lot deeper with clients and uses speaking as the way to introduce herself and those consulting services to them.

Type 7: The Jack of All Stages

This is a combination of other speaker types who use speaking as one of many revenue sources, which may also include books, courses, consulting, coaching, affiliate revenue, and more. Because they derive income from many sources, it's likely these speakers do not demand high fees for individual speeches but rather see speaking as a way to grow awareness for their other offerings.

Once you've determined what kind of speaker you want to be, it's time to take the next step, which is to begin expanding into new revenue sources.

ACTION PLAN

1. Calculate your Income Pie. Where is most of your income coming from? Do you spend the most time on those income-producing activities? Or do you need to cut out some things to spend more time on your most profitable efforts?

2. Decide what kind of speaker you want to be and focus on the activities that will help you get there.

> BONUS: For more help with diversifying your income, visit SpeakerBookBonus.com.

18

Creating Your First Product

At this point you should have a good idea of the financials of your business and may be starting to think about the different products and services you can launch to diversify revenue streams. Right now, it's easy to get overwhelmed because there are so many possibilities, and if you're excited, you may want to try them. But just because you can doesn't mean you should. There are plenty of ways to expand your influence and grow your business, but something has to come first. You have to pick a place to start and be smart about it; otherwise, you may end up wasting a lot of time, energy, and even money.

The key to picking where to expand your business first is to find out what questions, challenges, or obstacles your audience is facing, then create solutions to those problems. You need to help them achieve the transformation they are striving for. It's easier to sell something if you know somebody wants it than to try to convince them that they need it. If you know what questions your audience is asking, you can create something you know they want, so you'll want to do your research. Before you go through the work of creating an offering, find out what the market wants so you can first validate it.

Figuring Out What Your Market Wants

So how do you know what your market actually wants? There are plenty of ways to find out.

You can go to your audience. Your audience should be the first place you look to get inspiration for your products, either online or in person. For example, let's say for some of your speaking gigs you do a Q&A with the audience. What questions do they repeatedly ask you during this time or after you step offstage? There will be questions that come up again and again—pay attention to what they are. This is a good sign that there's an unmet need in your market, and there almost always is. Maybe they ask you about a book or course recommendations on a certain topic. Or they want you to more thoroughly explain a section of your talk on which you were unable to spend adequate time; they may want more details. These kinds of questions will tell you exactly what people are looking for.

You can go to your inbox. When people reach out to you via email, phone, or direct messages to ask questions, what do they ask you about? Sort through your inbox and see what kind of questions you get on a regular basis. What topics are those in your audience hungry for? What sort of resources are they looking for? As your influence increases and your audience grows, you will start hearing some of the same things over and over.

This is why I created my Beyond the Stage course: I had a lot of speakers asking how to expand their income, and I wasn't currently doing anything to answer that question. Make sure that you pay attention, because what people want may not be obvious to you. If you're good at something, and you do it all the time, it's hard to see why anyone else would need help with it. It may not seem like a skill or gift to you, but it is, so it's important to take your cue from others.

You can go to your network. Think about the different ways people you know ask you for help. Even if it's not directly related to something you speak about, is there something people are always asking your advice about? This indicates that your peers trust you with something. It's a useful cue that you have an expertise you may not even realize you have. Going back to step 1, you may want to consider other ways in which your expertise can be used to help people, beyond just speaking.

You can go to the internet. For example, scroll through Amazon looking for books on a topic you're interested in. Read the two- and three-star product reviews and see what people say. These are the reviews where people often share the unanswered questions they still have, whereas the five-star reviews are usually fans of the author's work and the one-stars are just trolling. But the two- and three-star people earnestly went looking for an answer, and somehow, the product came up lacking. Knowing where the author "missed it" on a given subject is a valuable piece of information even if you don't want to write a book.

You can go to big data. Instead of using your audience, which you may not even have yet, you can do some keyword research. Keyword research is great because it indicates real questions and challenges your ideal audience is searching for on the web. Start by searching who, what, when, where, why, and which for a given topic and see what autocomplete suggestions come up as you are typing those words in. Those autocomplete options are based on popularity, so you'll get an idea of what people are searching for. Then, scroll down to the bottom of your results to see what related searches people are using. You can also use tools such as Google Trends to explore the growth of various search terms over time, which can give you an idea of what areas are primed for growth.

When Melanie Deziel plugged "brand storytelling" into a tool called Answer the Public, she got a list of related search terms she hadn't even considered, which told her people were looking for more information on her area of expertise. With that information, she created a free digital guide to build her list and help her audience with what they wanted to do. Knowing what questions your audience is asking is essential to being able to adequately answer them and to eventually create an offering people will pay for.

The Competitive Audit

A great place to find inspiration for your products and services is from other people in your industry, which is called a "competitive audit." Here's how it works.

Start by identifying a list of ten or more speakers who speak on a similar topic as you do. They could speak on a slightly different topic, but they must speak to the same audience and be in the same industry as you. Make a list of their names, expertise, and websites. If there are any important differentiators between them, such as industry or background, note those differences because they may impact whether the product will be a good fit for you. For example, if someone speaks on a similar topic but only speaks to executives, it may make sense that they offer executive coaching. If your audience is not executives, then it's not a good fit for you, so be aware of the potential outlier effect.

Once you have your list, go to their websites and social channels to explore what else they offer other than speaking. What products and services do they have? Join their email lists, if they have one, and find out more information by becoming a subscriber to their content. What similarities do you see? Are they all authors with books listed on their websites? Are several of them promoting a course through pop-ups on their website? Are some of them offering coaching and consulting as well? Pay attention to all of this, because it can all be an indication of what opportunities are available to you. You want to do what seems to be working in this space—there's no need to reinvent the wheel—but at the same time not be a carbon copy of what they're already doing. The goal is to be similar but unique.

Then, observe the different price points of these offerings. This will tell you how much the audience values these types of products and services, which you will want to know when you decide whether to move forward with your potential launch of a similar product.

Once you've looked through all these speakers' offerings, spend some time thinking through what you've learned. Where is the "white space"? Where can you come in and offer something that meets a need without simply competing with what's already being done? Identify what opportunities exist for new and differentiated products and services and see what steps you can take to launch something that helps you achieve your ideal Income Pie.

Creating a Focus Group (and What to Ask)

Once you have a few ideas of what you want to create, you can get more direction by creating dedicated focus groups to learn more about people's needs and how you can help them. There are a few ways to do this.

If you want to test your audience's appetite for a specific product, you can create a digital survey. In the survey, include a few open-ended questions that allow for additional thoughts. Some of the best feedback will come from things you didn't think to ask that they include in the fill-in-the-blank sections of the survey. If you created an email list (which we mentioned in chap. 12 when we discussed setting up your website), you can send the survey to them. Otherwise, reach out to your list of previous clients and contacts, along with any friends or peers who can give you good feedback on this new project.

Another way to connect with people to discuss their challenges is to set up phone calls to talk with them directly and go more in depth on each question and answer. I recommend using a preselected set of questions to guide you, but let the conversation take its natural course. Of course this method is also limited by how much free time you have, but it often leads to unexpected insights you wouldn't get otherwise. To help add some scale to this method, you can use an online scheduler to allow people to choose a time on

CREATING YOUR FIRST PRODUCT

your calendar, which saves you the back-and-forth of having to arrange each call personally. Again, this is best done when you already have an email list of contacts to reach out to. It's difficult to scale a speaking business beyond selling your time for money without an email list of at least several thousand people.

The most personal way to get feedback and reactions from your ideal market is to meet with them in person, which will offer the greatest level of connection and spontaneity. Similar to phone calls, meeting in person will lead to unexpected insights as the conversation flows, but this method is also limited by your time and proximity to people. But if it's at all possible for you, this is a great way to look people in the eyes and get honest feedback on the next direction of your business.

What should you ask?

When interviewing people, you will want to keep in mind that how you guide the conversation will greatly affect its outcome, so be careful with leading questions. A leading question is one in which you're either consciously or unconsciously trying to get them to answer a certain way. "Don't you think product X is a great idea?" is an example of a leading question. It's clear you think the product is a great idea and want them to think so too, in which case they're more likely to say yes. Try to keep the questions open-ended in order to obtain honest and useful information.

Asking about what kind of product they want can be helpful, but be careful with this as well. Henry Ford has been quoted as saying, "If I had asked people what they wanted, they would have said faster horses." People don't always know exactly what they want in terms of a solution, they just know they have a problem. Try to aim your questions at gaining more information on the problem rather than the solution.

Other good questions include:

- Do you think this proposed solution would address your challenges?
- What value would you place on having this solution?
- How much would you be willing to pay for such a solution?

Answers to these questions will give you great insights on what people are struggling with, how you can solve their problem, and even what they'd be willing to pay for a solution.

Getting People to Buy: The Presale

When it comes to creating a product or service that complements your speaking, it's not enough to know if your audience wants it. They also have to be willing to pay for it. There are plenty of things people say they want that they're simply unwilling to buy. You may have asked questions in your surveys about what people are willing to pay for your product, to which some probably responded positively, but getting them to pull out their credit cards is an entirely different thing. To avoid your product crashing and burning, you can first validate the idea through a presale, meaning you get people to pay before you create anything.

CREATING YOUR FIRST PRODUCT

One way to do this is through crowdfunding. Whether you use a tool like Kickstarter or do it on your own, crowdfunding offers you a way to collect customers before your product is ever created or launched, so you know exactly how many sales you'll get at minimum and whether the effort will be worth your time. It also allows the audience to see a preview of your product and commit to pay ahead of time. Typically, this requires a minimum number of people signing up or investing a certain amount of money for the project to be funded. Because of this, not everything you sell is going to be a good fit for this presale strategy. Often crowdfunding is done for a physical or digital product that can be delivered upon completion, like a clothing or tech item; it doesn't work as well for service-based business offerings like consulting or coaching. Usually, these services are one-on-one and highly customized, so preselling to a mass of people is just impractical and frankly unlikely.

Another way to validate your idea is to simply presell the product or service on your own platform by collecting emails, commitments, and even payments from customers before the product is created. This is commonly done with online courses and programs when you give the audience an overview of what they'll learn and collect payment in exchange for delivering that course at a future date. I've done this with many of my courses in the past, gathering a group of students who will be a good fit for the program and agreeing to keep them updated on the creation progress. During this prelaunch phase, my team and I have shared course outlines with this group of people and received valuable feedback as we built it. In exchange, those people got early access to course material and usually an early-bird discount, and they were the first to take the course when it was finished.

The advantage of preselling a product is that you get to create exactly what your customers want, not just what you think they need. It also immediately gets cash in the door, which makes it easier to invest the time and money to build it. Once you have the money and committed customers who are waiting on you to build something, it lights a fire under you to get it done.

To make the offering compelling enough that people will actually pay for it before it's ready, you need to make sure that you have enough information about what people want. You need to have done all the earlier legwork that we talked about. You also may need to create a lot of material like excerpts, prototypes, or videos, and lots of copy explaining your process and what's to come. Don't let this scare you away from preselling. It's a great way to create and sell products. Just be sure that you are prepared to make the best possible case for your offering.

ACTION PLAN

1. Decide how you will discover what your audience wants. You could use surveys, Q&A at events, or phone calls.

2. Do some research on product offerings. Look at other speakers' websites, Amazon, or Google to figure out what products or services you can offer to help solve the problems of your audience.

3. Validate your idea through crowdfunding or preselling on your own platform.

> BONUS: For more help with determining what product your market wants, visit SpeakerBookBonus.com.

19

Selling from Stage and Other Ways to Monetize

Once you have something to sell, there are a variety of ways to get that offering out into the world. Depending on your topic, audience, and business model, you may be someone who incorporates product sales into your presentations. In this chapter, we'll cover how to integrate into your speaking any products or services you sell.

Whether it's a book, a course, or coaching services, first you need to know what you're selling and who it's a good fit for. Before you do anything, confirm with the client that it's okay to sell your product. Never assume permission. You will want to mention this to them early on in your booking conversations. In fact, I include it in my speaking agreement, and then at the event, I remind them again.

You actually have two audiences you can sell to: first, the clients themselves, and then the audience. If someone hires you for a keynote, one option to make more money and get more business is to let them know about your other offerings. You could say, "I know you hired me for this keynote, but I do additional trainings, like all-day seminars. Would you be interested in that?" If you do workshops, seminars, or consulting, mention those to clients who have hired you. Always look for other ways to add value for the client and your audience beyond the one thing they hired you for.

You can also presell your product to them, which I recommend doing whenever possible. Just as we learned in the previous chapter, when validating a new product to an audience, preselling something to people is an easier way to gauge how much product you will need and what the demand is ahead of time. I learned this with my first book, which I sold to individuals at high school speaking gigs. That wasn't easy for me, as I was often driving to many of the gigs and didn't know if I should be packing twenty books in the trunk of my car or two hundred, not to mention it was just a hard audience to sell to. Instead of trying to sell fifty books to fifty individuals, I realized it was much easier to sell fifty books to one person (usually the one who was booking me) who could then distribute them to other people.

One way to make this easier is to create speaking packages that include your various products. For example, you could offer a keynote and throw in one hundred books, or a keynote, workshop, and fifty books. Bundling your products and services together is a great way to increase your fee without having to take much more of your time. This goes back to your Income Pie and how you want to spend your time and make your money. Bundling also helps get your product into people's hands, which can help with word-of-mouth marketing, particularly when it comes to physical products such as books. You could also offer a discount to a client if they hire you and buy a certain number of books. In general, it's simpler to do a many-to-one model than vice versa.

If you do end up selling products at the event, what's called "back of the room sales," there are some common rules that can significantly increase your sales.

Rule #1: Give People a Reason to Buy Now

If people don't buy at the event, they most likely won't buy at all, so give them a reason to pick up your product while they're physically there. Create a sense of urgency by offering something you don't normally sell on your website or discount it significantly compared to wherever else they can get it. Make it an exclusive offer they can't get anywhere else and that is time sensitive to the duration of the event.

Rule #2: Sell during a Break

Make sure there's a break after you talk when people can buy. If people go right into another session, they're going to forget, so clarify this up front with the client and request a speaking slot before a break so you can maximize your sales opportunity. Try to find a place where you can set up a table in the back of the room right by a door to maximize foot traffic. In general, you want to be where most people will exit the room at break time, either inside the room or just outside so people can see you as they leave. If you're in a ballroom or auditorium, make sure you know where the main exit is or if there is some central place where everyone funnels out. That's where you want your table and products.

Rule #3: Keep the Pitch Short

In your speech, reference your products but don't spend a lot of time talking about them. You may have sat through presentations, as I have, where the speaker goes on and on about their products and the whole thing feels like one big sales pitch. Nobody likes that, especially the client, unless they have explicitly given permission to do this. Reference the product in passing during your speech, but make the pitch right at the end. Keep it short and sweet and let people know where they can find you afterward.

How long should it be? First and foremost, that depends on the client, so ask them what their parameters are. Again, never pitch something from stage without your client's explicit permission. In general, if you're keynoting someone else's event, try to keep the pitch to between thirty and sixty seconds. If you're selling higher-priced products and services, however, your pitch should be proportional to the length of your speech and the price of the product. If you're selling a $1,000 coaching package, it's acceptable for your pitch and explanation to be longer than for a $10 book. If you're doing a one-hour presentation, it probably doesn't make sense to do a fifteen-minute pitch; but if you're doing an eight-hour workshop, a fifteen- or even thirty-minute pitch may be completely realistic.

Rule #4: Use the Product in Your Talk

If you have a book, read a story or lesson from it onstage. I have a friend who does this a lot, pulling out his book and reading a funny story straight out of it. It's a short story, which makes it work as a stage prop that he includes in the talk. You don't want to read too much from anything scripted, but if you have a story that is written well, this is a great option to bring attention to the book without being salesy and to complement the content in your talk itself.

Rule #5: Do a Giveaway

Giving a product away can also be effective and strategic. Sometimes I'll give away a copy of my book to an audience member who has a birthday that day, or I'll ask a question and give a free copy to whoever answers first. This builds rapport and endears you to the audience. Plus, it's another great way to bring awareness to your products and to keep the audience engaged.

Rule #6: Use Product Packages

Creating product packages is a great way to sell more merchandise. When I used to speak to students, I would sell a book for $10, a T-shirt for $15, and a wristband for $1. But we would also sell all three items packaged together for $20. People may only want a T-shirt, but when they realize it's only $5 more for everything, they often go for it. Always have a package to sell that includes a bundle of various products and/or services, and be sure to mention it from the stage. It should be a no-brainer option that keeps the audience from feeling overwhelmed and gives them something simple that they can buy without having to think too much about what would be right for them.

In general, most speakers can double or triple their speaking fees when they include a product for sale at the event. Of course, learning how to do this is another craft in itself, but creating some products and services that take your work beyond the stage is an essential part of growth for almost every speaker. And if you're not offering those resources from the stage, you are missing out not only on more sales and money but also on being able to impact the audience in deeper and more significant ways. Selling from the stage doesn't have to feel slimy or sleazy; it's simply another way you can serve the audience, so you had better learn to do it well.

ACTION PLAN

1. Check with the event planner ahead of time to make sure you have their permission to sell your product. It's a good idea to consider putting this in your contract as well.

2. Decide what way of selling at events will be the best fit for your product.

REVIEW: STEP 5

1. Create your Income Pie and determine how much each source contributes to your overall income. What would you like to change?

2. Determine which speaker type you are.

3. Figure out what your audience and the market wants from you. Validate your idea.

4. Get your product out into the world.

> BONUS: For more tips on selling your product, visit Speaker BookBonus.com.

CONCLUSION

Six years after I decided to chase my dream of becoming a full-time speaker, I was about to step onto the largest stage I'd ever spoken from. The year was 2012, and this was a very different event from that first 4-H conference that kicked off my speaking career in 2007. It had been only six years, but a lot had changed since then.

That first gig in Missouri was for a small but respectable audience of a few hundred students. Now I was about to speak to an audience of 13,000 people. The event was in Oklahoma City, and I can still see it in my mind: the stage, the stadium filled with those orange seats, and that enormous light rig—all focused on me. Once again, I was both nervous and excited, but I knew I had put in the work and was ready for whatever came next.

Both of these gigs represent something significant to me. The first represents the opportunity, the chance to change my life and the future of my family forever. The second represents the fact that I had done just that. My life, and the lives

CONCLUSION

of my wife and daughters, had completely changed in just a matter of five years as a result of my decision to become a speaker. It wasn't easy, and there were plenty of sacrifices I had to make to get to this point, but it was all worth it.

When I stepped onstage that day at the Cox Convention Center, I knew I had made it in every sense. Thanks to a successful speaking career, my wife and I had been on life-changing trips together; my daughters had been able to see their dad do something he loves and were inspired in their own entrepreneurial efforts; and I was able to reach hundreds of thousands of people with a message that mattered. Since that moment, the momentum has only continued.

But for me, the meaning of the word *success* has evolved. Now, in addition to speaking, I have the joy and privilege of helping other people become successful speakers, and some of the most fulfilling parts of my journey have come from seeing others succeed in their own ways.

Like when Dr. Sue Ettinger crossed an item off her bucket list to take her family on a speaking trip to Maui. Never in her wildest dreams did she imagine such a fate, but now this is fairly common for her husband and kids to go on all-expenses-paid trips to someplace they've never been. That's success.

Or when Melanie Deziel quit her job at the *New York Times* to speak full-time and now consults with major organizations on how to use storytelling to build their brands. She uses speaking to connect with clients and help them do the deeper work of making their messages matter to a world that doesn't want to be advertised to but instead prefers to hear a great story. That's success.

CONCLUSION

Or when Erick Rheam recently emailed me (as I was writing this book) to tell me he crossed the $250,000 mark in speaking fees this year. That's success too.

All because of speaking.

That's why I share this message with you, why I haven't held back anything in walking you through the entire Speaker Success Roadmap. Becoming a successful speaker can change a person's life, whether your goal is to travel the world, make more money, or reach a wider audience with your message. For me, it was all of the above and more. I wanted to know my life had a purpose, to share my gift with the world, and to make a living doing it. And I knew I couldn't do that if I didn't understand the actual process to achieve success as a speaker.

I want that for you too. Whatever success means to you, and you are free to define it however you'd like, I hope this book helps you find your way. Keep following the Roadmap, keep doing the work, keep getting your message out there, and I'm confident you'll discover a life of deeper meaning and purpose. You'll become the communicator you were meant to be—a truly successful speaker—and the world will thank you for it. Now go make your message matter.

ACKNOWLEDGMENTS

Bringing a book to life is a journey, and journeys are best taken with others. This book has certainly been a long journey, but it didn't get to this point from my efforts alone. There are so many people who helped make this possible.

The person most directly responsible for this book is Jeff Goins. It all started with a text I got from Jeff a few years ago that simply said, "Have you ever thought about writing a book?" That led to many discussions, meetings, a book proposal, more meetings, Skype sessions, a rough draft, a few more meetings, many emails, and finally this finished product that you have in your hands.

Jeff took my content from course materials, podcasts, blog posts, interviews, webinars, and interactions with students and created the manuscript. He, and our phenomenal collaborator, Liz Morrow, did an amazing job of taking my existing content and fleshing it out into its final form. Jeff tolerated my constant questions and guided me through the entire process. Sometimes it's dangerous to do projects with

ACKNOWLEDGMENTS

friends, but I would go on this journey all over again with Jeff.

At the beginning of this project, Jeff connected me with Chad Allen, who would eventually become our editor for this book. I told Jeff I was only interested in this project if he and Chad were both involved. Chad made me excited about the prospect of creating this book and helped me see the vision of how it could impact so many speakers.

My biggest fan and supporter is my wife, Sheila. She believed in me when we were young and poor and I said I wanted to chase the crazy dream of becoming a speaker. She's incredibly patient, loving, encouraging, and supportive of whatever endeavor I want to attempt. To love's eternal glory, Pal. ;-)

I am always grateful for my parents. To my mom, Cristy, for being the most positive and encouraging person on the planet and for being excited about anything I do in life. To my dad, Dave, for instilling in me an entrepreneurial spirit and strong work ethic. My siblings, Taylor and Kelsey, are also pretty cool and inspire me with their own creative entrepreneurial pursuits.

As much as I love being a speaker and entrepreneur, my favorite role is being dad to Sydnee, Emilee, and Mylee. I absolutely adore my daughters and am thankful for their daily reminder of what matters most in life.

Huge thanks to Brian Vos and the entire Baker team. I am incredibly grateful for all your work behind the scenes to bring this book to life.

There were so many mentors and speakers early in my career who helped support and inspire me. Thanks to Phil Boyte, Jason Dorsey, Scotty Gibbons, Monty Hipp, Judson

ACKNOWLEDGMENTS

Laipply, Rhett Laubach, Kyle Scheele, Josh Shipp, Josh Sundquist, Harriet Turk, and Jeff Yalden.

Thanks to so many professional speakers, entrepreneurs, and friends who have supported me and The Speaker Lab on this journey: Ian Altman, Jane Atkinson, Scott Backovich, Jay Baer, Trivinia Barber, Nathan Barry, Joshua Becker, Ty Bennett, Jenny Blake, Chandler Bolt, Bob Burg, David Burkus, Adam Carroll, Steve Chou, Kyle Chowning, Dorie Clark, Joey Coleman, John Corcoran, Hugh Culver, Andrew Davis, Ryan Delk, Chris Ducker, Brandon Edmonson, Ray Edwards, Brian Fanzo, Pat Flynn, Thomas Frank, Erin Gargan, Vinh Giang, Casey Graham, Tim Grahl, Shawn Hanks, Jordan Harbinger, Clay Hebert, Patrick Henry, Todd Henry, Jason Hewlett, Greg Hickman, Michael Hyatt, Neen James, John Jantsch, Mitch Joel, Jeremy Johnson, Phil Jones, Kent Julian, Noah Kagan, Mike Kim, Matthew Kimberly, Amy Landino, Bob Lotich, David Loy, Jaime Masters, Patrick Maurer, Scott McKain, Mike Michalowicz, Dan Miller, David Molnar, Arel Moodie, John Michael Morgan, Nick Morgan, Mike Pacchione, Michael and Amy Port, Ryan Porter, Clint Pulver, Cliff Ravenscraft, Mark Sanborn, Tim Sanders, Liz Saunders, Marcus Sheridan, Thom Singer, Pamela Slim, Alan Stein Jr., Shawn Stevenson, Scott Stratten, Jake Thompson, Ron Tite, Andy Traub, Bob Upgren, Pete Vargas, Scott Voelker, Jon Vroman, Wes Wages, Aaron Walker, Nicole Walters, Tamsen Webster, Carrie Wilkerson, Alli Worthington, and Omar Zenhom.

Special thanks to several close friends who supported this project from the beginning and have been great sources of encouragement and wisdom: Jon Acuff, Bryan Harris, Joseph Michael, Jeff Rose, and Shane Sams.

ACKNOWLEDGMENTS

Today at The Speaker Lab, we have the privilege of teaching and inspiring speakers all over the world. I'm simply one small piece of that puzzle. Our team includes Dan Alia, Emily Arnold, Christie Buckner, Katie Campbell, Rachel Chandler, Rick Clemons, Conrad Close, Brandon Compton, Andrew Davis, Charles Forest, Zach Forner, Maryalice Goldsmith, Ryan Hacker, James Haynes, Sam Hill, Nanette Hitchcock, Kyle Houston, Melissa Howard, Dan Irvin, Katherine Johnson, Jim Kukral, Josh Mathis, Michelle Onuorah, Alan Peck, Brittany Perkins, KC Procter, Ravi Rajani, Erick Rheam, Brittany Richmond, Jeremy Rochford, Morissa Schwartz, Chris Seo, Ron Smith, and Jake Thompson.

CLAIM YOUR FREE RESOURCES

Thank you for reading *The Successful Speaker*! To claim your FREE bonuses, please visit:

SpeakerBookBonus.com

Grant Baldwin is the founder and CEO of The Speaker Lab, which has trained over 10,000 speakers since 2015. He is also the creator and host of *The Speaker Lab Podcast*. A popular keynote speaker and entrepreneur, he lives near Nashville, Tennessee, with his wife, Sheila, and their three daughters. Visit www.TheSpeakerLab.com for more information.

Jeff Goins is the bestselling author of five books, including *Real Artists Don't Starve* and *The Art of Work*. He lives with his family just outside Nashville, Tennessee. His website, www.goinswriter.com, is visited by millions of people every year.

Printed in Great Britain
by Amazon